African Mythology

Journey Through Time With Myths and Folklore

(A Captivating Guide to African Mythology and Gods of Ancient Egypt)

Paul Beeson

Published By **Harry Barnes**

Paul Beeson

African Mythology: Journey Through Time With Myths and Folklore (A Captivating Guide to African Mythology and Gods of Ancient Egypt)

ISBN   978-1-9992555-8-9

No part of this guidebook shall be reproduced in any form without permission in writing from the publisher except in the case of brief quotations embodied in critical articles or reviews.

Legal & Disclaimer

Table Of Contents

Chapter 1: African Gods

Katonda: Creator God of Baganda People

The honoured name that the Baganda people, who notably speakme stay in what is now Uganda, use for their remaining author god is Katonda. As a part of their rich manner of existence, the Baganda humans love Katonda and word him as the father and the chief in their pantheon, which they call the Balubaale. The Buganda humans in East Africa worship Katonda as their author god. They see him as the daddy of all gods and the king and the determine of the sector. Usually, Katonda is shown as an unknown, all-encompassing stress. Despite this, some stories say he ought to possibly tackle a human-like hide with darkish pores and skin and an extended beard. It has additionally been encouraged that he positioned on a white dress and a royal crown to reveal his purity and power.

Katonda is regularly visible due to the fact the most critical and lone god within the Baganda oral manner of life. Because of this, he has no own family members like humans do. But inside the Baganda pantheon, referred to as the balubaale, precise gods or spirits are seen as divine and have precise jobs or trends. Most of the time, the ones balubaale aren't taken into consideration as Katonda's direct own family individuals. Instead, they may be taken into consideration part of the larger spiritual order or divine council.

Katonda is often seen as a father and head of the Balubaale, representing his function due to the fact the Baganda people's creator and dad or mum. It's critical to keep in mind that Baganda mythology and spiritual ideals can range among people and agencies, so there can be distinctive techniques of knowledge those relationships. Katonda's relationship with the possibility balubaale seems more hierarchical than familial.

In the Baganda manner of life, Katonda has many names and developments. In the sky, human beings call him Lissoddene, because of this "the notable eye." He is also called Kagingo, which means that "the grasp of lifestyles;" Ssewannaku, due to this "the everlasting;" Lugaba, due to this "the giver;" Ssebintu, this means that "the draw near of all topics," Nnyiniggulu, which means that that "the lord of heaven," Namuginga, which means "the shaper," Ssewaunaku, due to this "the compassionate," Gguluddene, which means "the first rate one," and Namugereka, because of this "the distributor."

Within the conventional Baganda faith, Katonda is preferred for having many effective inclinations that show he is the maximum crucial author god. He is concept to have created the world with all living matters, this is considered truely one in every of his major inclinations. With his divine strength, Katonda has the super power to create and offer life to everything. This is how the Baganda humans see the universe.

One of the most crucial components of Katonda's individual is his omnipresence, due to this that he's constantly there inside the international. The Baganda discover comfort and route in the reality that he's everywhere at all times. This technique that he constantly maintains the arena in balance. He furthermore is privy to the whole lot, it honestly is referred to as omniscience. This manner he is aware of the whole lot approximately the past, the prevailing, and the destiny. This offers his fans a experience of divine information.

Because he's seen because of the reality the protector and figure of the Baganda people, Katonda additionally has protection talents. This aspect shows how type and being worried he's because he cares about the fitness and happiness of all of the living topics in his international. Katonda is the "draw close of existence," which means that he's carefully connected to the life energy that maintains all living matters going. This clarifies his function as a god of care and annoying.

In addition to being a protector, Katonda is likewise called the lord of heaven, which means that that he recommendations over the spiritual international and has complete power. As a god, he can exchange people's and businesses' fates and provide benefits and suitable good fortune. This suggests how deeply he is involved within the lives of people who serve him. Finally, a few debts of Katonda stress how big and terrific he's with the aid of calling him "the big one." This gives to the respect and awe that the Baganda humans have for him.

Also, African diaspora religions have made a distinction. These religions integrate African spirituality with Christian and neighborhood practices. People in religions along side Santeria, Candomblé, and Vodou worship gods or spirits. Many of these religions come from African religious practices. In the places wherein they're practised, the ones blended-religion religions have impacted art work, song, and society.

Also, academic packages that goal to preserve and unfold traditional African customs and beliefs have received tempo. Scholars and organizations paintings tough to maintain the ones customs alive as an critical a part of African subculture with the useful resource of writing them down and training them to new generations. It's possible that native African religions and gods are not not unusual these days. However, they're nevertheless important to many African groups. Their effect is growing, making humans worldwide more aware about and respectful of Africa's many customs and non secular ideals.

Anansi: Trickster God

Anansi is a decide from oldsters memories who looks like a spider. Many humans keep in mind him as a god for records. He has additionally been stable as a trickster, a element that comes from West Africa. The man or woman is stated to be a trickster who can beat sturdy combatants through manner of being modern and clever. Even notwithstanding the reality that he performs a trickster, his deeds make him frequently seen because the primary character. People in West Africa often inform spider reminiscences, but the Anansi recollections come from Ghana. They spread to one of a kind places, similar to the Netherlands and the West Indies.

"Anancy" or "Ananse" are a number of the specific names and bureaucracy Anansi is verified in literature. Even although he's typically demonstrated as an animal, he additionally may be anthropomorphized as a human face on a spider or a human body with spider-like dispositions like eight legs. In many fairy memories, Anansi has a family. In some places, his wife Okonore Yaa is referred to as Aso, Crooky, or Shi Maria. His specific kids are Ntikuma, Tikelenkelen with the massive head, Nankonhwea with the willing legs, and Afudohwedohwe within the pot belly. In a number of his memories, he also has a little one named Anansewa.

In folklore, Anansi is regularly set up as taking factor in exclusive gods' sports activities activities, and those gods frequently deliver him supernatural powers. In a few memories, he is even visible due to the fact the son of the Earth Mother. People from distinctive nations from time to time call him a lesser god. In Akan's faith, he is often seen as a prophet, but his enthusiasts do no longer see him that way. They have amusing him as an possibility as an historical healer, a sign of knowledge, and the individual that made the initial human body.

Rather than being a sign of defiance, he grow to be frequently visible as a signal of staying alive. This is because of the truth he turned into smart and sneaky enough to get lower back at the people hurting him. Slave Africans decided that tales about Anansi gave their lives a revel in of continuity, which helped them get up for who they had been irrespective of the reality that they have been being held captive.

The awesome way to pay interest memories approximately Anansi modified into to pay attention to them, and he became notion to be the maximum modern and professional speaker. Over time, this exercise grew to encompass superb types of fables. Tales were additionally brought to the the rest of the arena with the resource of way of slaves added for the New World thru the Atlantic slave trade.

Because there have been such masses of Ashanti slaves in Jamaica, their stories and proverbs are normally better acknowledged and more correct. People called him "Kwaku Anansi", even supposing he became a slave. The Akan call for Anansi is "Kwaku." Anansi modified into vital to Africans in masses of techniques, not absolutely as a slave owner. He has moreover modified proper into a decide visible as a traditional hero.

AFRICAN GODDESS

Oshun: Goddess of Love and Freedom

The Goddess of love, liberty, fertility, and water, she made the arena and healed it collectively together with her powers. The Orisha tale says that Olodumare, the handiest god, despatched Oshun to earth to make a worldwide with male gods. Her darkish in shade, lovely, and flirty appears went properly with the acute gold dress and the sparkling earrings she wore. The male gods concept Oshun grow to be lovely however did not suppose they wanted her assist to make the area. She got indignant that nobody regarded to care about her, so she left and walked to the moon, wherein she stretched out and checked out herself within the reflect, know-how that they could soon need her help.

After a brief time, the Earth dried up. Animals and plant life were death, and lifestyles grow to be coming to an quit. The Gods have been lost when they went to Olodumare; they failed to recognize what to do. When Olodumare noticed that Oshun wasn't there, he scolded the Gods, telling them that Oshun modified into essential for Earth's survival. Earth would possibly now not exist with out her love, splendor, and power to make lifestyles. The Gods went again to Oshun and begged her to come returned back.

Being the type Goddess that she was, she did, but not earlier than telling them they must by no means mistreat her once more. The Earth have become yet again doing nicely at the equal time as she have been given lower returned. Women who have the identical energy as Oshun are strong, impartial, and type these days. They love with out problems and recognize how extensive relationships are. These girls are pleasant and beneficial but in no way be a victim.

Oshun is the best Orisha that is in no way mentioned in those memories. Different money owed of her story say that she is each Yemaya's daughter or her extra younger sister. She is the smallest of the Orishas. At the begin of time, when Obatala finished with the primary paintings, it despatched 17 Orishas to land to make things right and cease Obatala's mission. There had been seventeen of them, and 16 of them were men.

The guys did not pay attention to her recommendation on making lifestyles sweet, adorable, and substantial, in order that they failed at their goal. They needed to be humble and tell Olodumare the lousy facts. When they had been given there, they were requested wherein their 17th Orisha became. When they admitted that that they had overlooked her, they had been advised they couldn't stop the artwork without her and had to ask her forgiveness another time. God completed making the arena by using giving it love, fertility, and beauty. He made everyone want those items, that have turn out to be advent's give up.

At this element, Oshun did no longer have her realm, collectively with the opposite Orishas did, because of the truth she modified into despite the fact that very more youthful. Shango was in rate of lightning and fireside, Obatala changed into in rate of the sky, and Ogun become in fee of metalwork. Each of the alternative Orishas cherished their area of strength. Oshun turned into journeying the arena for some time while Ogun discovered how lovely she changed into and started out to comply at the side of her. She fell proper proper right into a river at the identical time as on the lookout for to break out from him and changed into being sucked down thru the cutting-edge-day at the same time as Yemaya noticed her and stored her. She gave her the existing of sweet water and rivers as her area so she must continually have an oasis to name domestic. After that, Yemaya became however the parent of water, however Oshun emerge as in price of freshwater, in particular the Osun River.

After this, the Orishas were sad in Olodumare because of the reality the ruling beings once more, similar to earlier than. They concept they may run the area higher. Esu knowledgeable the very top notch being that the Orishas may also not do what they have been informed, so Olodumare ceased the rain. There grow to be a horrible drought that dried up all of the water our our bodies on the land. The earth started out out to die. The Orishas knew that they had disappointed Olodumare and begged him to forgive them, but he each would no longer pay interest or couldn't.

Oshun became a peacock and flew to Orun, excessive in the sky, to inform Olodumare that the Orishas had modified their minds. But the enjoy changed into lengthy, and he or she had to flow very close to the solar to get to Orun, which harm her feathers and made her lose lots of them. Even no matter the reality that she changed into tired, she stored going until she ultimately fell into Olodumare's hands as a buzzard. Because she modified into courageous, determined, and willing to sacrifice, Olodumare healed her, allow the rain fall, and made Oshun the fine Orisha who may additionally additionally want to maintain words to Orun from then on. Because of this story, the peacock and vulture have turn out to be related to her.

She stated she helped make the location and spared it from extinction. However, human beings are also proven to smash existence when they hurt her thru being careless, merciless, or not respecting the holy and natural international. As the goddess of easy water, she could be capable of forestall it from raining to make it dry or send an endless wave to scrub away folks that upset her. In the Yoruba rendition of the Flood of Creation story, the Orisha Olokun fills the arena with water from the sea due to the reality Obatala took an excessive amount of land at some point of the creation manner. In this version, Oshun never does whatever to punish the people for their sins.

Aside from her occasional tantrums, Oshun is tested to be type, merciful, and sound. In one tale, people who lived thru the river Osun close to the metropolis of Osogbo left out her simple requests and have been washed away. But folks that came later seemed and honoured her. In trade, Oshun promised to protect, manual, and offer for them, which might assist Osogbo growth. The metropolis changed into related to Oshun and come to be seen as a holy spot in which human beings want to skip on pilgrimages. In her honour, the Osun-Osogbo Fair remains held every one year at the Osun-Osogbo Holy Grove out of doors the city. People tour from each corner to pay their thanks.

People think that Oshun stored her phrase to the primary individuals who respected her on the location via stressful for present day-day pilgrims' ailments and wounds, making them fertile, making sure healthy births, and helping people with their many life problems. People be given as genuine with she is a goddess who is acquainted with how hard it's far to undergo adjustments. Since she is related to transformation and the issues that encompass loss or exchange, she moreover comforts believers who grieve and those on the lookout for to start a current existence.

On the alternative hand, Oshun has a person and might misbehave, much like people do, which makes her even more approachable. Shango's first spouse modified into Oba, and his 0.33 spouse modified into Oya. In one story, Oba asks Oshun to make an truely certainly one of a kind meal for Shango, and he or she or he falls in love with Oba. Before making the meals, Oshun wraps a headband spherical her head to cover her ears. Then, she gives a mushroom that resembles an ear to her meals and offers it to Shango. Shango likes it. Oba thinks Oshun reduce away her ear on the identical time as getting prepared the meal, so she does the identical detail the subsequent time she makes it. She serves it up to Shango, who feels angry and turns it down. After that, Oshun and Oya make fun of Oba.

People normally recollect Oshun as a being of properly deeds, mild, luminosity, goodness, and kindness. This story offers him a human aspect by way of the use of way of showing that even the excellent people can misbehave, which makes human beings more likely to forgive each other for their errors. She is associated with the peacock as a sign of change, the vulture to demise, rebirth, statistics, and resolution, the skunk to independence and protection, the otter to playfulness and happiness, and every butterflies and bees to fertility, and happiness, in addition to exchange.

As an entity that allows with converting states, Oshun can help with a huge type of troubles, together with women's reproductive health, digestive nicely being, non secular and highbrow fitness, or even issues that men have with the same matters. She come to be one of the maximum famous gods in West Africa because of the reality really everybody desired her. This reputation observed her at the same time as her subjects have been taken across the sea to the New World in opposition to their will.

Chapter 2: Goddess Of Weather

The climate goddess is idea to be one in every of humanity's maximum important. There have been three types of Olodumare, and she or he have become one of them. Goddess Yemaya, the Great Sea Mother, gave beginning to Oya and her brother Shango. But it's far no longer clean that their father have become. Some critiques say that Oya changed into now not pregnant. One day, she is said to have made an providing out of a holy material with the colours of the rainbow. The material then gave begin to 9 children, four units for twins and one named Egungun. That's how people known as her the "mother of 9."

People moreover take delivery of as genuine with that Oya need to make subjects right amongst males and females. They can name in Her to try this. Her blade or sword is used to make room for emblem spanking new boom, this is some other name for her. She is idea to watch the newly deceased and assist them change from existence to loss of existence. It has ties to the Vodou Lwa Maman Brijit and, like Oya, watches over graveyards.

Oya can fast and reliably bring about alternate. Oya has a tendency to return and make you exchange matters when you have emerge as too occupied, exhausted, or a massive located-provide. The Goddess states that you need to dig up the floor earlier than you could plant some thing and that change normally gives you with what you want to grow to be entire.

Ala: Goddess of Earth

Ala is the Earth Mother Goddess in Odinani. She is the female Alusi of the earth, morals, death, and fertility. She is the earth's mother goddess, the draw close of the underworld, the protector of the harvest, and the goddess of each human and animal fertility. People from Nigeria known as her "mother of all things." At the begin of life, she brings toddlers into the arena even as their moms are despite the fact that pregnant. At the end of life, she takes the souls which might be lifeless into her very private belly.

A snake or a bee's nest is idea to be a signal that Ala sends to her clergymen to expose them in which they might gather a Mbari. Building the constructing takes years of hard work with the useful resource of groups of males and females, and it's miles seen as a sacred act. The homes are left to crumble after the Mbari is built. The Mbari habit is probably passed on with the aid of using more youthful humans in the group so long as new homes are constantly being constructed.

She additionally entails a desire what is proper and incorrect for humans and is on top of things of Igbo regulation, it truly is referred to as Omenala. People who do terrible things to Ala are recommended that they insult her, it without a doubt is why she is called no Ala. Lighting candles is a famous way to honour Ala. If you moderate a flame inside the early hours and greet Ala and spring, people assume you will be blessed with many youngsters and contemporary mind.

AFRICAN MYTHICAL CREATURES

Inkanyamba: Giant Snake With Horse Head

In South African folklore, the Inkanyamba is a tale approximately a massive snake with a horse head residing in a water frame close to Pietermaritzburg. The folks who live inside the region think it's miles a scary creature this is most busy inside the summer season. The tale of the

Inkanyamba comes from pictures observed in caves in the KwaZulu-Natal region. People have referred to as the ones animals "rain animals" due to the fact they seem during storms.

There is an animal referred to as the Inkanyamba that lives in rivers and lakes. It's taken into consideration extra than 20 ft prolonged and looks like a snake or an eel in every manner besides for its head, which seems like a horse. A lot of the time, human beings say that the top seems like that of an animal, like a horse or a zebra. The monster is said to private a mane on its decrease again that looks as if a fin and a mane on its head that seems like a horse.

People receive as proper with that seasonal storms and high winds appear because of the reality a male Inkanyamba can not locate an appealing lady who furthermore lives within the depths of a unmarried river. Scientists think the Inkanyamba is associated with the Anguilla marmorata and the Mossambica. These freshwater eels can broaden up to six ft lengthy, however the human beings there say it isn't always right. They suppose it's far masses larger and has magical powers. According to a story about the Inkanyamba, it's far domestic to a large tornado inside the summer season. The Xhosa humans say this creature can fly like a huge hurricane to find out a mate. They are also linked to the disappearance of family animals for no apparent cause.

Aboriginal rock artwork within the course of the KwaZulu-Natal vicinity display that people knew approximately the ones animals extended within the beyond. Archaeologists are starting to call the ones drawings of animals "rain animals" because of the reality they may be frequently seen throughout excessive summer season storms. Most researchers anticipate that the Inkanyamba are a massive species of freshwater eel, much like the Anguilla mossambica or Anguilla marmorata, that could boom about 6 ft prolonged. However, the those who stay in the place say that the Inkanyamba are a good buy larger and function some everyday tendencies.

People within the KwaZulu-Natal areas of Ingwavuma and Pongola blamed the deadly Inkanyamba for a horrible hurricane that destroyed lots of homes as late as 1998. The fact that the reptile is rarely seen inside the summer season has added about this vintage link with the Inkanyamba and awful climate. Traditional Xhosa perspectives say that the Inkanyamba is going up into the sky every 12 months within the shape of a big tornado to find out a mate.

Although there are neighborhood ideals that they'll be not gift inside the summer season, the Zulu have prolonged notion that those animals migrate due to the reality they may be now not visible during that time. Wildlife like these has been visible alongside the Mkomazi River, forty 4 miles southeast of Howick Falls, and inside the water that swimming swimming pools at the Midmar Dam. Smaller dams near fields in the Dargle area in the Midlands have additionally been said thru humans who've been there. Even more exciting, there had been debts of Inkanyamba preventing violently inside the water over who owns the territory. Others who noticed the rituals say they stuck quick glimpses of them happening.

The animals first were given global limelight in 1996, whilst the close by newspaper presented an incentive for certainly everyone who might also want to provide photos of the creatures. Two photos have been posted, but neither in reality showed what the animal seemed like, and they had been later idea to be fakes. The massive debate about whether or not or now not or now not or now not these creatures exist became handiest made worse with the resource of these images.

Just three hundred and sixty five days later, within the Mzintlava River region, it truly is near Howick, there was a similar debate approximately the lifestyles of a few other massive aquatic predator. People who lived there stated they were being attacked via a huge crocodile with an extended neck and a proboscis that could pierce through the skull. They called it the "African Brain Sucker", or Mamlambo in the close by language.

There changed right into a rumour in May 1996 that the South African authorities ought to capture the animal under Howick Falls and skip it to an environmentally covered place. This brought on severa media interest. People in the vicinity who're Zulu had been livid about the plan and asked their nearby council to step in, but no longer for the motives that PETA lovers may additionally moreover assume.

Those who lived there feared that the people sent to trap the beast won't be geared up to cope with the chance. The violence need to unfold to shut via villages if the Inkanyamba's anger could not be contained. According to the present day statistics, the South African government has changed its thoughts approximately getting into opposition to those powerful semi-aquatic animals on their domestic turf.

Chapter 3: Hybrid Serpent

The god Damballah looks as if a snake. The universe have become made through the usage of his seven thousand coils, which make him the precise existence pressure. He original valleys and mountains on Earth along with his coils and stars and planets in space. After making the arena, he shed his snakeskin to make all the water on Earth. In Vodou, water and rain are connected to lifestyles, and while God made the seas, he made it feasible for life to start. All living topics get strength from him like water emerge as made from his lifeless snake pores and skin. She is his spouse and is referred to as the Rainbow Serpent. They are normally demonstrated collectively within the pics, and she or he helped him purpose them to. They every needed to appear for introduction to take region because of the truth, in Vodou, introduction is some thing that a man and a lady do collectively. The loa who live in

Damballah and Ayida-Wedo are the oldest and wisest. They constitute increase and promising change, just like snakes do. When a snake loses its pores and skin, it changes right right into a notable animal.

He is part of Rada nanchon of loa, due to this that "guardians of order, morals, and ideas." As the deliver of all motion in lifestyles and power, Damballah permits preserve the sector going. He lives in the sky and wraps his coils throughout the Earth, continuously dropping his pores and pores and skin. He sheds his pores and skin to make rain and floods, which convey life-giving water to the land. He is the ruler of all knowledge and offers human beings intelligence and information. Because he can see into the beyond and destiny, Damballah tips over intelligence and understanding. The past, the prevailing, and the future are all tied together with the aid of him. Because of this, he's regularly associated with the lifeless, which affords some one-of-a-kind respected thing to this well-known loa.

People reflect onconsideration on Damballa as stunning, moderate, sensible, and sort, however not concerned in the troubles that humans face each day. He brings peace simply by way of the use of the usage of being there, and he's a continuum that is "right away a reminder of the beyond and a assure of the future." Because he is so antique and a snake, he can not communicate. But he can whistle or emit a easy hissing sound. During a rite, a serviteur concept to be seized via the use of Damballa moves to the floor like a snake. He come to be given a white sheet and had each different one waved to kick back him off. His purity is so high-quality that it can't be introduced to subjects that are not herbal. Some peristyles maintain a bowl of water that the possessed will soar into to swim and take a seat backtrack. People supply him milk, white materials, vegetation, coconut, rice, orgeat syrup, and a cologne referred to as lotion Pompeii as items. But his splendid dish is a white egg that isn't always cooked sitting on a pile of white flour.

Damballah exists inside the sky, but you can furthermore discover him in lakes, streams, and ponds. Many church houses have ponds internal them simply so Damballah can stay there. Damballah is usually easy, and he stays away from folks who are grimy or ill. Ensure that every one the fans who come to the ritual are clean and healthful due to the fact Damballah won't come inside the occasion that they may be now not. For some loa, smoking and eating are constantly allowed and welcome at some stage in rites. But for him, smoking and eating aren't allowed all through rituals. If worshipers want to name on precise Loas at a few degree inside the workout, they need to attend to smoke and drink until Damballah has left. On March 17, his banquet day, human beings get carrying white and inexperienced, jump in streams, and swim in lakes and ponds. He is given sugar, white flowers, silver, chickens and eggs and loves they all. Damballah is a welcome a part of all of us's life. However, he in particular appears out for disabled human beings, parents which can be white, and little kids.

When people name on Damballah, and he is taking over, he does now not speak or glide like a person. When Damballah rides a devotee, the devotee flicks his tongue, creeps along the ground, and climbs tall topics. These snake-like actions show how effective he is across the groups. He is hidden in the again of a easy white linen even as he has someone in his possession to guard his privateness. Damballah does now not speak, whistling and hissing like a snake as an alternative. Only Papa Legba can translate his hisses into human language. People count on this because of the fact Damballah's expertise is so extraordinary that we can't apprehend. Even so, having the giver of lifestyles round at some point of rituals is good as it brings peace and organization spirit!

Like severa different loa, Damballa is made from numerous spirits with special jobs. Damballa Tocan, as an example, is an entity of the mind. It is Damballa La Flambo on the equal time as he indicates up inside the Petro rites. Ayida-Weddo is Damballa's partner, however in some Vodou businesses, she is his sister. In others, she is Damballa himself in each other way. Again, Erzulie Freda modified into his lady buddy, however in a few cultures, she might be seen as his spouse.

The wonderful Voodoo god Damballah and his partner Ayida are examined as a rainbow inside the sky. He is also validated with the aid of way of using an air of snakes related to each specific, which stands for sexual group spirit. Regarding Earth, the smaller Damballah, Simbi, is thought to feed springs and rain. People additionally name Dan Petro the "stern snake that lives up the tree." This is a few aspect that the slave mutiny that made Haiti a free territory in 1804 left within the again of. Even despite the fact that they have names that sound like enemies, the cosmic snakes of Damballah, Petro, and Simbi aren't. St. Patrick is associated with the Damballah Wedo god, who sent snakes to the ocean. In traditional artwork, Damballa is confirmed as a huge white snake. This photo comes from Wedo, now called Ouidah, in Benin. He could have been the number one object Gran Met made.

In some Vodou companies, Ayida-Wedo is married to Damballa. In specific memories, his bond with Erzulie Frederica is one-of-a-type. Even although they have been together in advance than, she should now be taken into consideration his partner. Damballa can be called Damballah, Dambala, Dambalah, and masses of different strategies. Some Vodou companies do not forget that Damballa represents the Sky Father and the initial character who made all dwelling topics. It is said that he used 7,000 strands to make the universe's stars and planets. He additionally normal Earth's hills and rivers.

By dropping the snake's pores and skin, Damballa need to make all of Earth's waters. By transferring back and forth amongst land and water like a snake, Damballa brings lifestyles to the world and makes it complete. He's often linked to Moses and Saint Patrick. People think about Damballa as type, thoughtful, and affected man or woman. However, he is also unaffected through people's every day troubles and troubles. Because he's so vintage, he cannot communicate, however he can emit a mild hissing sound like a snake. He stands for a line that connects the past and the destiny.

Children's Play uses Damballa's name for the primary terrible man, Chucky, who uses voodoo spells to transport his soul to the body of the Good Guy Doll. In Sierra, the principle individual, Gabriel Knight, works with the primary character to treatment a string of killings. Sadinar, the High Priest, places Damballa below the snake god.

Chapter 4: African Vampire

According to their story, the Ashanti folks who stay on Ghana's Gold Coast have a witch who can remove one in all a kind human beings's lives and energy. Obeying is the word for that person. These people say that that is a few thing that humans develop up with and can not pass directly to others. The obeying is considered human, however his mystery won't be saved if he gets attacked in public considering that they supply off phosphorescence after they revel in threatened. People who workout this form of witchcraft are said to have creepy eyes and be loopy approximately meals. People say that once they'll be shifting, they're capable of offer off phosphorescent moderate from their anus and armpits. Like Asians, they are capable of alternate form, fly, and hunt at night time.

People frequently take into account the Obayifo, a awful witch who takes benefit of people's worry and unhappiness. A few names, along with obeyifo, asiman, and Asanbosam are privy to it. However, there are some versions among them. A few subjects approximately the Obayifo make it special from special vampires, even though it feeds on the veins of harmless youngsters. One factor is that Obayifo is a stay element possessed by way of an evil spirit that makes it do bad matters. The excellent people who can inform them apart are the Okomfo and White Wizard. They move about their lives as neighbours, pals, hubby and better halves. An Okomfo, a holy monk, is the handiest character who can guard you from an Obayifo. Some may say he worships the Obayifo and may defend himself from it with magic and charms.

This phrase is used to provide an reason for folks who devoted witchcraft in the Ashanti place. These human beings are referred to as obeying. But this word can be used for both folks who completed this form of witchcraft and people who became to monsters. People who practised this shape of witchcraft are particular from people who changed into monsters because of the fact this shape of witch is most effective used on men at the equal time as becoming monsters is handiest used on women. People assume the obayifo is connected to African vampire magicians because of the truth they're fabricated from phosphorus. Even even though it's miles frequently called a vampire, an obayifo differs from the vampires in Europe. People think about it as an evil witch that feeds on people's unhappiness and worry. This watch is likewise referred to as asiman, asanbosam, and obeyifo.

Because the witch is so hungry, she leaves her body at night time, and the obayifo flies off to find out her meals, typically kids and vegetation. She likes the cocoa tree, too, which makes chocolate what it's far. Getting rid of someone's lifestyles stress may require an extended length, and the man or woman may not die for numerous days. When the obayifo beverages a paranormal liquid crafted from fruit and veggie juices, it could exchange into specific animals that it is going to make use of to assault human beings.

The Obayifo can also disclose its frame at night time time as a colorful orb that glows or a burning fireball to do evil matters, that might damage human beings or their flowers. That leads us to every special interesting issue about the Obayifo: it eats stop end result and veggies, too. It enjoys using blight to damage cocoa flora. If the Okomfo stops him from eating the children's blood, he can wait as prolonged because it takes to stay alive on plant sap. What's even stranger is that the Obayifo are believed to glow through their armpits similarly to anus when they exit at night time. I do question suppose the Okomfo can tell the distinction among an Obayifo and someone else. However, I think that closing trait can be a useless giveaway. But it is just me.

An Obayifo is also recognized for having "shifty eyes," which I don't have any concept what this means that. People had been regularly known as Obayifos, despite the fact that, if they have been feeling jealous of someone else, if a number of their youngsters handed away or in the occasion that they might no longer deliver food to people walking thru. People believed they have been sufferers of the Obayifo while their vegetation got ill, if their youngsters were given malaria and tuberculosis, or even as a person internal their circle of relatives died due to the Okomfo's guarding. Interestingly, the Obayifo in no manner take kids in their blood; they'll be clearly concept to have a mild snack. However, saliva is assumed to be fatal as it's wherein ailments and ailments come from.

There are also certainly considered one of a type tales about how a person becomes an Obayifo. Some say that Obayifo is born with their powers, on the identical time as others say it's far a curse or that they could get it with the beneficial useful resource of eating or ingesting blood from humans or flesh. The matters that render Obayifo particular furthermore bring about accusations and superstitions quite some the time. If a person became suspected of being an Obayifo, they'll simplest be killed through drowning or being strangled with the aid of an Okomfo. If you have got been a vampire, it end up a wonderful demise. The tale of the Obayifo modified into an exciting one all spherical. There are but locations in Ghana in which people worship antique spirits and deities with the help of a Shaman. While the obayifo isn't a zombie, it's miles a stay aspect that an evil spirit introduced decrease returned to lifestyles. Most of the time, it is tough to inform whilst this creature is round due to the fact its enterprise is so close to. People assume that the obayifo can best be advised what to do by a White magician, shaman, or Okomfo. People suppose the Okomfo is the handiest aspect to guard them from the witch.

Yumboes: African Elves

The Wolof humans of Senegal, West Africa, stay on the coast near Goree Island and feature memories approximately fairies referred to as yumboes. They are two toes immoderate and have a silvery white shade inside the direction of. People suppose they're the souls of the deceased and shape near bonds with human households. They live within the ground, under the Paps hills. The name "Paps" comes from the truth that many hills global appear like a girl's breast. Some had been stated in Senegal, like the Deux Mamelles. The Yumboes live in fancy houses in which they cover appropriate feasts. However, they consume with the resource of the usage of taking human food and sporting it off within calabashes. They acquire their fish, at least.

The Wolof human beings in West Africa take delivery of as genuine with in magical beings referred to as Yumboes. People anticipate that they will be ghosts which may be related to people. They live at the Paps hills. People from anywhere in the international have visible those hills, which look like a lady's breasts. It is said that the Yumboes, which may be toes tall and silvery white, are the souls of human beings who have died. People experience near them, and their hair is regularly stated to be silver.

A woman who lived on Goree Island, placed off the west coast of Senegal, knowledgeable him approximately the living matters. She said a Wolof maid advised her about them. Keightley says that the creatures appear to be fairy creatures from Europe. In addition, they appearance masses like African ghosts. "yomba" comes from a Wolof word for "pumpkin," that is related to the idea that yumboes need to steal meals from human beings. Keightley says that is a hyperlink between the Wolof humans and the coolest humans of Europe. His one-of-a-kind name is Bakhna Rakhna, because of this "correct human beings" in English.

The creatures inhabit the hills near Paps and devour at massive tables with assist from folks that cannot be visible except for his or her ft and hands. Whenever they have a awesome feast, they name foreigners and locals. Even despite the fact that the Yumboes stay in fancy houses, they nevertheless consume human nourishment, which they scouse borrow from human beings and perform on calabashes. They trap their fish, however.

Chapter 5: African Mermaids

The story of mermaids has become well-known anywhere inside the globe. However, the African fluid spirit of Mami Wata has been respectable and honoured given that earlier than African countries met Europeans. She remains respected in West, Central, and Southern Africa and among her human beings who have moved to the Americas. In the African religion for Voudun, she end up taken into consideration considered one among its most powerful gods. Today, she is respectable as a goddess you have to love and worry.

Aphrodite, Ishtar, and Astarte are some of the opportunity historical mermaid goddesses who are considered immortal spirits representing opposites. These can be beauty, danger, natural strain, recovery, wealth, destruction, health and infection, and a failure to have a look at ideas for efficiently and evil. She is as strong, volatile, incredible, sexual, and capable of kill a few detail in her manner as the ones historical mermaid gods.

Over the years, her African lovers did no longer suppose heaps specific about her. She is regularly confirmed as a pretty mermaid with prolonged hair who is half of human and half of fish. But every so often, she could be capable to stroll on land in a extra human frame. Her earrings and garments are continuously present day, colorful, and difficult to copy. She is frequently visible with a small reflect-coiled snake around her head, breasts, and waist. This wealth represents the wealth and beauty that her fanatics can gain.

Interestingly, her pores and pores and skin is honest and moderate, which isn't always normally seen in African gods. African human beings located a amazing deal meaning into the colours that Mami Wata wears. The color red stands for blood, violence, and dying, while the color white stands for faith, beauty, and the girl body. She is usually proven naked in her mermaid form, collectively together with her lengthy hair combed back and her eyes consistent at the golden mirror.

All over Africa, humans have informed memories approximately assembly the Mami Wata. The most famous tale says she lurks close to the water and steals women and men as they swim or are on a ship. When the captive goddess thinks they are well worth of her love, she will be able to convey them again to shore dry and with a brand new view on faith and religion, frequently making them rich, cute, and well-known. People she met say she left her comb and reflect in the the the front of sailors. She may also preserve coming decrease returned to them in their dreams once they took the matters and ask for them lower back in change for sexual favours forever. People who worship her in Africa and the diaspora positioned on her traditional red and white garments, offer her highly-priced foods and distinct matters which might be notion to carry wealth and experience her dance and song that located people in a trance-like country. At those events, humans don't forget Mami Wata can take over the dancers and communicate to them, wishing them a happy, healthy, and fertile existence. She is, but, blamed for masses horrible subjects taking region inside the sea, as are all water-primarily based gods. People in Cameroon despite the fact that anticipate that the sturdy undertow currents that run close to their coast kill swimmers who get stuck in them.

Were-Hyenas: Shapeshifting Hyenas

The had been-hyena is a kind of therianthrope, which means a completely geeky phrase for a person who can exchange right right into a residing factor or a human-animal blend. It's no longer a surprise that the animal in query is a hyena. It's moreover no longer a marvel that the story comes from North Africa, wherein hyenas are simply as regularly occurring as irritated English human beings on the Underground in London. But do no longer genuinely write off the have been-hyena as an African version of our favorite werewolf—they're lots more complex than that.

In assessment to werewolves, who're super human beings that coronary heart, had been-hyenas start as both human beings that may trade into hyenas or, extra unusually, as hyenas who can fake to be human beings. In assessment to werewolves, were-hyenas may be each male and lady. This makes them the stereotypical gay werewolf. Being a were-hyena is a two-manner avenue that outcomes in horror. They once in a while hunt on my own, but now and again in corporations, as if having animal energy and a in no way-ending starvation for human meat wasn't horrifying sufficient. At night time time, they may be mentioned to name humans's names to tease them and get them to move away protection, in which they may be attacked and eaten. You may want to possibly want to deliver a bat for baseball with you the following time you pay attention your mom calling you down the steps, definitely in case.

People concept that magicians and witches ought to alternate into these animals each time they preferred. But every other unusual African perception stated that blacksmiths were basically responsible for had been-hyena assaults due to the truth they were idea to be more likely to turn into those animals. This went too a protracted manner in Ethiopia, in which human beings concept that all metalworkers were bouda, witches or wizards who've to change into hyenas whenever they preferred. Ethiopian Christians frequently said that Ethiopian Jews had been bouda due to the fact they spread rumours that they ate Christian our our our bodies that they observed within the ground. Most people think that one idea came from the alternative because of the fact Jewish men inside Ethiopia were often blacksmiths, which made the 2 connections very smooth.

Being which have been-hyenas continuously had strength over their transformation, they may show up every time, but they preferred to alternate at night time. They are blacksmiths, so at the same time as they may be not stalking their prey, they've a reputation for doing all styles of disgusting things, like stealing from graves, ingesting animals, stealing things, and making horseshoes.

In the Kunari tongue of the antique Bornu Empire, which covered masses of the land spherical Lake Chad, they have been referred to as bultungin, meaning "I exchange proper right into a hyena." At some element, this brought on some of call confusion because of the reality people have been no longer positive if they were being charged with being a hyena or if their pal grow to be telling them they have been one. People used to count on that the ones animals inhabited some villages within the place, like Kabultiloa. This is probably why the house costs have been so low.

Some Berber people reflect onconsideration on them as guys or ladies who grow to be hyenas that night time time and decrease decrease back into people in the morning. As some distance away as Persia, people stated a monster referred to as a kaftar that became "1/2-guy, half-hyena" and loved to kill youngsters. In Greece, up until the flip of the century, human beings idea that the ghosts of werewolves that were not accurately killed may want to go back to battlefields as vampire hyenas and drink the pus of troops who have been death. In brief, people within the beyond concept hyenas have been...Jerks.

A hyena man with mouths that could speak and chunk concurrently modified into each one-of-a-kind viable form of the had been-hyena. A magician may additionally need to show genuinely all people who had eaten human meat proper into a hyena guy; therefore, preserve an eye constant on all your pals who consume human beings. It have become said that they desired dwelling near cemeteries and eating the flesh of the deceased. However, similarly they loved consuming the flesh of live human beings. Some appearance wonderful, regardless of the reality that they have got mouths, and a few appearance bizarre and scent like hyenas. If you examine any handsome men with foul mouths on Tinder, be prepared to swipe left.

It is said that the were-hyena can change into 3 specific paperwork: someone, a human-hyena hybrid, and a hyena. As people, they look masses such as you and me, however perhaps with a fashionable Mohican to make matters greater exciting. They can handiest drift on their decrease once more legs due to the fact they may be crosses. Their faces look like hyenas', and their huge golden eyes glow purple rapidly before they assault. Upon without a doubt converting into Hyenas, they will be a whole lot large than their real species and every now and then don't have any fur. They are said to smell like rotting meat and have been referred to to kill the sufferers alive in advance than coming to go back later to consume their our our bodies.

People belief the have been-hyena changed into the exceptional way to reveal how scared and angry they were of hyenas in real life. Were-hyenas had been humans and hyenas in order that they could exchange into humans and hyenas. There are myths and records in the again of the hate we revel in in the course of our furry buddies. Some of their features appear to trouble us in critical processes. They are active at night time, it is surely scary because it approach they're able to see us even as we can't see them. Their one-of-a-kind yipping sound, like hysterical humanity laughter, is terrifying and may have made humans assume they could talk human language and contact people with the aid of call.

It is now in particular verified that they kill maximum of the animals they consume. However, within the beyond, they have been idea to be scavengers who ate useless animals, which made them appearance both cowardly and disgusting. In conventional African reminiscences, they were even blamed for stealing our bodies from graves, hurting human beings's souls, gathering human remains and displaying them as prizes, stealing youngsters, and deceiving humans for fun."The Dispersal of All Animals" is a fantasy from the Beng inhabitants of the Ivory Coast. It tells how Hyena, the horrible man, attempts to get the opportunity animals to homicide the first guy and lady who ever lived. In many methods, the dog is the alternative of the Hyena. Luckily, the dog warns our ancestors earlier than they are killed and wiped out of lifestyles.

Hunters although kill hyenas each yr due to the reality they'll be believed to kill horses, dig up graves of humans who've died, and bite off the legs and arms of youngsters who sleep outdoor. It may additionally additionally appear like a no-brainer, but kids must not sleep by myself in the barren area at night time whilst risky hyenas are round. Some Arab folktales even stated that hyenas were vampires whose eyes can also want to appeal humans or their hormones need to make them need to bite them. We want a sprig of that Sex Hyena in area of that Sex Panther.

In a few instances, this dislike of animals have grow to be related to and made worse via manner of the hate of a selected organization, like Jews or blacksmiths. This may additionally were a starting shape of anti-Semitism. Many of the myths' records have been likely primarily based at the wealthy statistics of Africa's many close by folks religions. It would possibly possibly have even come from dread of the Korè cult, a collection of Bambara people from Mali who tried to "grow to be" hyenas with the resource of dressing up as them and playing position-gambling video video games. To placed it every distinct way, the horrifying recollections about have been-hyenas might have been due to means of furries.

Chapter 6: The Creation Saga

The putting commonalities taking place in herbal religions across the world rise up from the reality that every one peoples had been confronted with the same crucial stimulus from the sunrise of humanity. The solar and moon, the earth and sky, the factors, the eternal cycle, and the animals of nature all begged the same query to shape the superb and compound mystery. From this important mystery springs inexplicable systems of veneration and worship that, however minor close by versions, personal commonplace troubles. The maximum famous polytheistic society in Africa, the ancient Egyptians, were ruled with the aid of using Ra, the sun god, who merged with Amun-Ra to shape the "Hidden One," the immutable and imponderable god of gods. The notion of a solar god is intuitive, for even the maximum primitive intelligence can confirm the number one nature of the sun inside the cycle of lifestyles. Thus, the endowment of that phenomenon with divine houses may need to appear quite herbal.

Africa comprises some 12 million rectangular miles. It is over three times the scale of Europe and debts for 22% of the landmass of the arena. A considerable percentage of it's miles barren region, inclusive of the high-quality sand ocean of the Sahara Desert (protective some three.Five million rectangular miles), further to the Namib, Kalahari, Nubian, Turkana, and Somali Deserts, which together upload a comparable place of uninhabited or moderately inhabited regions to the complete. South of the Sahara, there lies the Sahel, an area of semi-barren region, populated in large part with the useful aid of pastoral nomads. The tropical areas stretch from the Atlantic coast of West Africa, the Bight of Benin, and thru the basin of the Congo River. To the east and south lies the savanna belt, stretching south as an extended way due to the fact the southern peninsula. One of the maximum large, herbal features of Africa is the Great Rift Valley, which commences in the Levant and reaches as a long manner south because the Cape. However, its maximum recognizable capabilities are the deep valleys and volcanoes of the primary Rift, concurrent with cutting-edge-day Tanzania and Kenya, overlapping into the Great Lakes location and the continental divide.

Africa, as isn't always unusual understanding these days, represents the cradle of humankind wherein evolutionary threads of the human species separated from the apes. As the sciences of archaeology and anthropology keeps to find out the earliest origins of mankind, sparkling reveals are but periodically unearthed, which includes the oldest hominin fossil determined in Africa thus far, which come to be unearthed in the deserts of Chad in 2001. The extra ultra-modern movement and distribution of the human species across the face of Africa is notably less hard to devise thank you, at the complete, to the take a look at of linguistics. To plot this in all of its element, of course, could be not possible in a piece of this length, but viable draw a massive delineation into six primary language families. Afroasiatic languages are those spoken finally of North Africa, the Horn of Africa, and elements of the Sahel; the Austronesian languages are those spoken in Madagascar; the Indo-European languages, introduced through way of European colonists and regularly the lingua franca of massive areas nowadays, is generally in pidgin shape; the Niger-Congo and Bantu languages are the maximum extensively dispersed; and the

Nilo-Saharan languages are spoken in places together with Sudan, Chad, and Mali.

As the Christian religion little by little marched in the direction of domination of the Roman Empire, the symbolism have grow to be that of Christ. In Coptic and Ethiopian Christian imagery and iconography mainly, many Ancient Egyptian beliefs had been repurposed for the sake of Christianity. This is plain in the enigmatic, twelfth century Lalibela Churches of Eastern Ethiopia in which Pagan and Christian symbolism are every freely used at a time whilst one faith superior to dominate every one-of-a-kind. The notion of Christ as the son of God merging with the super and almighty God, the only God, is uncannily just like the merging of Ra with Amun-Ra to create a better caste of divinity.

Africa changed into delivered to Christianity starting with the Copts of Egypt, which stimulated the installed order of Ethiopian Christianity, which manifests in recent times within the Lalibela Churches. As is the case with Abrahamic faiths, their introduction into Pagan lands, the ones societies running toward shamanism or animism, took place manner to an overlap of ideals and a crucial compatibility among faiths. Today, Africa is dominated with the aid of the Christian faith, added in sub-Saharan Africa by using European missionaries at the dawn of the imperial generation. The cannons of Christianity proved properly matched with the fundamentals of African notion structures. Barring the suppression of witchcraft, polygamy, and such devilish practices as drumming and dancing, the missionaries determined it noticeably smooth to convert massive numbers of black Africans. Historians element to the destruction of indigenous African society because of slavery and colonization, but many skills of present day-day African Christianity include strong, residual elements of traditional African religions.

The concept of God because the all-effective, all-expertise creator of all subjects is a not unusual sufficient subject matter in the African religion for Christian missionaries to make inroads. African folktales, in particular those seeking out to provide an reason behind natural phenomenon such and the solar, moon, and stars, forever function the intervention of a notable being. However, previous to the creation of Christianity and Islam, the belief in a monotheistic God have become an alien notion. This is proper insofar because the traditional African view of the ideally suited being have become, and is, naturalistic, but there may be constantly something present on the middle of the universe that is singular, all-effective, and immutable. Notwithstanding numerous, inevitable nearby variations and one-of-a-type names, the similarities are regularly extra placing than the versions.

In a nutshell, within the broader, full-size enjoy, the African view of the very outstanding being is usually indistinct and sick-formed. The perfect being is form of commonly faraway and dissociated from the more elemental, every day human observances. It is a phenomenon that can not be understood, and there are so few who nonetheless subscribe to animism to waste time attempting. The global of ancestral spirits is far extra present and right away, and wherein a theocracy or priesthood exists to talk and interpret the message of the ideal being, its paintings is arcane and past the records of commonplace men.

Onyangkopon of Ghana, Ngai or Kenya, Mwari of Zimbabwe, Ruwa of Tanzania, Nkulungkulu of South Africa, and a high-quality many others all describe the lifestyles of a outstanding being. The presence of this ideally fitted being, as with the Abrahamic God, permits account for the more facts of creation lying past the tangible realities apparent to the senses. Numerous names for, and definitions of, "God" have been chronicled by way of manner of anthropologists over the years, however few if any definitive motives have been provided as to the nature of that divinity. All that emerges is a head-scratching feel of neither expertise nor being mainly inquisitive about anything that element might be, however it does no longer usually intervene within the every day lives of earthly ladies and men. The African best being isn't always the God of Islam and Christianity, worrying worship and veneration, however a few element completely disinterested inside the minutia of often going on life; the duty of localized phenomenon belongs to a bewildering plethora of natural spirits.

Variations at the mythological man or woman of the perfect being are not first-class local but localized, without a two people inclined to agree even as asked. Even in terms of advent myths, the concept that the fine being created guy alongside all of the creatures of the earth, and actually, the earth itself, isn't everyday. In the case of Mulungu, for instance, the commonplace Malawian name for the great being, legend tells of that being having requested from in which all the beings and creatures wandering the earth have come. In precise versions, the human species emerged from some spontaneous generation, at the same time as the animals are referred to as "Mulungu's people" in contradistinction from mankind.[1] Sometimes, the call of this ideally fitted being is similar to the call for lack of lifestyles. Not on occasion, demise as a phenomenon is in some way linked to the paintings of a closing being.

All of this consequences in the problem of introduction myths and testimonies which range pretty from vicinity to place and way of life to manner of lifestyles. The advent myths and stories of Africa are such numerous and varied that we're capable of most effective touch on a handful right here. Most, in a single way or a few different, are formed with the beneficial resource of the herbal factors in life round an character humans or interlinked company of peoples. The Nile, as an instance, glaringly knowledgeable the historic mythology of Egypt, and Mount Kilimanjaro encouraged the arrival fantasy of the WaChagga people of northeastern Tanzania.

The maximum extensively allotted African language business enterprise with the useful resource of an extended manner is that of the Bantu. The tale of the Bantus' dispersal is one of the maximum interesting sagas of African information. In a phenomenon referred to as the Bantu Migration, or as cutting-edge anthropology has an inclination to decide upon, the Bantu Expansion, the Bantu race radiated outward from its deliver to dominate an entire lot of Africa by way of using the usage of manner of incremental migration over masses of years. It would possibly, possibly, be honest to observation that most outsiders consider an "African" in terms of the ordinary "Negroid" or "Congoid" kind, making up the fantastic preponderance of African populace. These are the Bantu.

The Bantu originate in the area of the Niger Delta, bordering present day Nigeria and Cameroon. Sometime spherical 1,000 to 2,000 BCE, pressures on land and the later improvement of Iron Age technology triggered a constant, outward enlargement. In its handiest phrases, the movement unfold west and north however more vigorously east and south, moving first to occupy the crucial areas of the Congo Basin earlier than crossing the continental divide and moving into the conduit of the Great Rift Valley. This channeled the migrations north and south, eventually allotting the Bantu language all through maximum of east-applicable Africa and exceptional swaths of the south. During the direction of this decorate, extra ancient Neolithic races have been displaced, absorbed, or assimilated. The satisfactory massive surviving instance of this are the Bushmen or San of southern Africa who took safe haven within the arid west of the subcontinent, wherein small pockets live on to nowadays.

It is expected that over 1,000 exquisite languages are spoken in Africa, with many hundreds of associated dialects. The Congo, the most important African united states of the united states of the united states, is domestic to over 325 remarkable languages and masses of extra dialects. Often, the proper Bantu root become not unusual through extra historic languages, and clearly, the contemporary languages of South Africa show the robust have an impact on of the "click on" style of the San. Then, there are languages along side Swahili, a Bantu language at its root, however precipitated with the useful resource of Arabic and Indian vernacular delivered through worldwide alternate with the east coast of Africa. It have become used as the Swahili lingua franca of change in huge regions of the indoors and dispersed the language as a common medium of communique, regularly as a second or 1/3 language, across maximum of Africa's east-vital place.

This southward movement of the Bantu brought with it atypical myths and legends related to the historic origins of the race, with many more gathered alongside the way. As a effect, the mythology and folklore of Africa are dominated via Bantu stories and legends.

The nearby attention of cultural mythology has an inclination to test the density of population, and the maximum massive concentrations of the population have historically been in the tropical areas. Anthropologists have moreover stated that wooded vicinity lifestyles and studies will be predisposed to generate a mainly dense and colourful mythology over the years, associated with the a protracted way more variety of existence pervading the wooded region. Forests moreover will be inclined to restriction bodily imaginative and prescient, and in a worldwide of deep recesses, darkish shadows, and such a form of natural form, nature spirits proliferate with equal abandon. West and Central Africa are seemed for mask and fetishes. Deeper superstitions emerge among wooded area corporations, and lives have a tendency to be lived in ordinary intercommunication with unseen spirits of the wooded region.

Pre-colonized African society changed into a society in which the information end up archived inside the tradition of storytellers, and it is thru this medium that the mythological foundation of any human society is mounted. Song and dance furthermore occupy a place inside the every day device of lifestyles, with specific songs and dances appropriate for every seasonal profession and each social feature in society. The recording of the oral way of lifestyles sooner or later of Africa started out out out throughout the turn of the 20 th century and continues to at the existing time, in spite of the truth that the density and vivacity of the African oral manner of existence have dwindled to remnants underneath the have an impact on of modernity.

The urge to recognize the arena and the machinations of nature has typically been strong. In Africa, as is the case some place else, the advent myth is the important function of social identity, and there are as many versions of it as there are man or woman societies and organizations inside the societies.

Perhaps the maximum quoted introduction myths in encyclopedias of African mythology are those of the Yoruba, one of the essential language businesses in contemporary Nigeria. From the Christianized south to the Islamized north, Nigeria gives up what is possibly the broadest cultural and ethnic range in Africa, possessing a awesome intensity of innovative and literary historical past. This story is informed in masses of variations at some stage in Yorubaland, universally beginning with the moves of the Olodumare, or great being. Olodumare had sons, the first, named Obatala, and the second, Odudwa. One day, Olodumare despatched his sons to earth, giving them three topics to keep: a bag, a chook, and a chameleon.

A commonplace feature of every model of this story is that at the time, the earth have become made from handiest water and no land. In multiple version of this tale, divinities accompany Olodumare's sons to Earth to put together the land or create it on the water's floor. In others, it is determined that the land is contained inner a bag, first inside the form of sand upon which a coconut palm is planted, and secondly, black soil interior which the primary flowers are sown. Meanwhile, Obatala, the younger of the two brothers, discovers the coconut palm's functionality to provide wine, which he drinks after which falls asleep. Oduduwa, the older brother, opens the bag and discovers the sand, which he spreads at some point of the roots of the palm tree. He then releases the chameleon upon the floor of the sand. With the slow and careful gait of a chameleon, it determines that the beach is proper and enterprise enough to go through weight. Next, the soil is unfold out, and the chicken is launched. As hens are apt to do, she vigorously scratches and issues the soil, spreading it gently, growing the land.

Soon sufficient, Oduduwa ventures to check the integrity of the land himself. As he does, Olodumare sends Prosperity down as a gift to him. Prosperity is normally depicted as girl who brings in conjunction with her seeds for cultivation, a bag of cowrie shells for trade, and three iron bars to be stable into knives, axes, and hoes. Thus, Oduduwa emerges because of the reality the number one king of Ife, the first u . S . A . Of Yoruba, on the same time as Obatala stays the numerous palms and becomes a drunkard.

Nigeria have become one of the first areas in Africa to come lower back underneath the have an impact on of every Christianity and Islam. Christianity arrived on the coast with the primary missionaries, at the identical time as Islam grow to be added from the north thru trans-Saharan trade. As a give up result, Nigerian introduction myths were changed beneath the effect of the Abrahamic way of life, because of the reality the person of conventional great beings were tailor-made and rationalized to fit the Christian and Islamic notions of God. In Nigeria, as in each British colony, human beings on trial or giving testimony in a court docket of law swore an oath to considered one of their conventional deities with their hand on a Christian Bible.

A version of the Yoruba advent tale follows the same essential trouble, insofar as above there has been pleasant sky and below, quality water. The sky modified into dominated via manner of way of Olorun even as his partner, the goddess, Olokun, ruled all that become underneath. This time, the hero is Obatala, a minor deity who requested and turned into granted permission from Olokun to create the earth for the usage of dwelling creatures. Obatala descended to the earth, bringing with him a gold chain upon which to climb all of the manner all the way down to earth, a snail's shell entire of sand, a white fowl, a black cat, and a palm nut, all of which turned into carried in a bag. The sand turn out to be unfold, and the white chicken launched to scatter it about. Obatala referred to as the region Ife and dug a hole to plant the palm nut. As he waited for a wooded region of palm wood to broaden, he saved agency agency with the black cat with whom he occupied himself, fashioning creatures out of clay. He have come to be under the influence of alcohol on an intoxicating drink made from the palm, and the creatures he had crafted from clay, the people of the land, were imperfect, because the human race remains these days. This angered Olokun who initiated a excellent flood.

In the savannah areas of the south is the maShona u . S ., a majority tribe in modern-day-day Zimbabwe. The term "maShona," it's far probably really worth noting, isn't one which constantly originated within the tribe itself. Today, it stands as an umbrella term for a dispersed organization of individual clans and sub-agencies, sharing a collective language and lots of common cultural trends, but who do no longer regard themselves as a unified people. The call have become completed by way of the second primary tribe of Zimbabwe, the amaNdebele, a near blood and ideological relative of the Zulu, and until the colonial duration, the militarily dominant of the two. The maShona introduction tale, regardless of its essential commonalities, varies in element during a spectrum of clans and sub-clans. Nonetheless, the maximum normally referred to version tells a poignant love story between the earth and the heavens.

Mwari, the right being of maShona mythology, created Mwedzi, or the moon, in a deep pool of water. Characterized as male, Mwedzi implored Mwari to allow him to stay on land. To relieve his loneliness, he became despatched Hweva, the morning famous individual, to be his spouse. This, Mwari agreed to do, upon the records that Hweva would go back to the firmament after years. In those years, Hweva conceived and gave starting to all the plants of the world. After years, Mwedzi returned her to her domestic inside the sky as promised, with profound reluctance. Soon, he come to be lonely again. This time, Mwari despatched him the midnight film star, Morongo, every so often Venekatsvimborume, underneath the identical situation: that she ought to go again in years. Venekatsvimborume, too, conceived, giving beginning to all the peace-loving birds, animals, and people of the area. However, at the same time as the time got here for Morongo to return, Mwedzi must no longer permit it.

Morongo right now conceived once more, this time giving start to the violent predators: lions, crocodiles, toxic snakes, and stinging creatures, like scorpions and wasps.

Mwedzi and Morongo's future end up for every of them to go back to the sky, in which they keep to live to at the present time. The elements of this tale satisfy the question of earth and sky, the former temporal and the latter divine, together with the procreation of high-quality and evil. It furthermore touches at the importance and veneration of water and its divine strength for amazing and evil. Water capabilities prominently in network maShona mythology, an example of that's the initiation required of a novate spirit medium to stay underwater for severa years in advance than rising with the internal-imaginative and prescient essential to talk with the God and the spirits.

Another example of the recovery power of water can be visible in a story explaining the difference among black and white. During the era of colonization, the curses of slavery and inequality were manifestly seen in a racial context. Whites, with their overwhelming electricity of technology, wealth, and moral authority, had been visible as blessed via God, while blacks, the issue of oppression, bondage, and misfortune, were seen as prone and cursed. It became told that a pool of cleanliness existed wherein Mwari ordered the humans to easy. Those who had been fortunate to find out the pool whole of water emerged white, whilst the ones arriving later to find the pool nearly empty had been simplest able to wash the fingers in their arms and the soles in their toes.

The story of Unkulunkulu, the ideally suited being of the Zulu, is a lot much less complex, and in a few respects, extra human, for Unkulunkulu derives from a human shape. The Nguni, comprising the Xhosa, Zulu, Ndebele, and Swati sub-groups, are a Bantu those who originate inside the japanese location of South Africa. The Nguni had been widely scattered in the direction of the forestall of the 18th and early nineteenth century via way of the advent of the Zulu wars. As a impact, Nguni languages are spoken in areas as dispersed as Zimbabwe, Mozambique, and Malawi, with a similar dispersal of Nguni folklore and mythology.

Long in the past, because of the reality the tale is going, the earth existed first-rate in darkness with not some thing however a unmarried seed representing lifestyles in its latent form. At some component, beneath unwell-described occasions, the seed sank into the ground, and from it emerged a large mattress of reeds, known as "Uthanlga", or the source of all things. As time handed, a unmarried reed transmuted into the shape of someone, named Unkulunkulu, the "First Man" and writer of all matters. In time, precise reeds started out to become men and women. Others grew livestock, fish, and wild animals. These Unkulunkulu plucked off their branches and let out on the land. He then created the mountains, rivers, valleys, wind, rain, solar, and moon. He taught the humans to domesticate, prepare dinner dinner, hunt, and make fireside, and he named every and each creature of the earth.

Chapter 7: A Depiction Of Mbombo

There are numerous variations at the problem depend of God's growing man from clay, originating in each corner of the area. In Greek mythology, Prometheus lengthy-set up men from clay, as did the Egyptian god, Khnum. A variant of the Yoruba introduction story sees Obatala developing mankind from clay, and comparable subjects are located in cultures as widely dispersed because the Māori and Inca.

One such tale is recommended by using the Shilluk human beings, described as a Luo Nilotic people of South Sudan, living on each banks of the better Nile. The perfectly suited being of the Shilluk is Juok, who molded all of the human beings of the world from clay. While he became involved on this art work of creation, he perplexed the region, locating clay in the land of the white man, and from this regular the white race. In Egypt, alongside the banks of the Nile, he encountered red dirt from which he made the brown races. Lastly, when finding his manner to the land of the Shilluk, he came upon the rich black earth in which all topics growth, and from that, he created the black race.

As he sat with a lump of clay before him, Juok notion to himself, "I will deliver men prolonged legs to run inside the shallows at the identical time as fishing, like the pink flamingos; I will deliver them extended fingers to swing a hoe the way a monkey swings a stick; I will supply them mouths to consume millet and tongues to sing with; and I will offer them eyes to appearance their food and ears to pay interest their songs."[2]

Other southern Sudanese versions tell of God baking his clay women and men in a bread oven, leaving them goodbye they burned, developing the black race. Trying all over again, worrying now not to make the same mistake, he eliminated them from the oven early, and that they've been underdone, consequently developing the white race. Trying for a third time, he succeeded; from this emerged the terracotta-coloured human beings of the brown race which he considered satisfactory. They had been, therefore, legal to stay inside the fertile regions of the Nile.

As modified into genuine with the River Nile, the remarkable geography of a selected panorama regularly knowledgeable the mythology of the people residing upon it. As has often been the case at some level inside the records of mankind, mountains are endowed with super importance. Wherever a brilliant mountain is present, a deity continuously is residing upon it. In Kenya, the Kikuyu deity, Ngai, occupies the summit of Mount Kenya, at the same time as Ruwa, the God of the Wachaga human beings of northeastern Tanzania, lives on Mount Kilimanjaro.

Table Mountain, seemed to the Khoisan as Hoerikwaggo, because of this "mountain in the sea," is the signature feature of the southernmost African city of Cape Town, and the residence of Qamata, the fine being of the Khoi. While busy developing dry land out the sea, a sea dragon, known as Nkanyamba, tried to prevent him. A fantastic battle followed in which 4 awesome giants joined on Qamata's side. When the struggle become over and the dragon defeated, the giants had been grew to emerge as to stone, forming the competencies of the mountain. The largest become given the choice Umlindi Wemingizimu, or "Watcher of the South," and it have emerge as Qamata's home.

The Great Rift Valley is home to Africa's most mountains and numerous important lakes, amongst them Lake Tanganyika, Lake Victoria, and Lake Malawi. Along the jap shore of Lake Malawi is dwelling a people referred to as the Yao, a department of which might be also coastal dwellers who've been in contact with Arabic customers for generations. They are, consequently, predominantly Muslim, however that does not prevent factors of ancient way of life and faith of their folklore and mythology that live apparent nowadays. It is their notion that inside the earliest times, their conventional god, Mulungu, lived on earth in a circumstance of peace and masses. Death and cruelty had been unknown till within the future, a chameleon built a fish lure which he dropped into the river. The following morning, the entice became entire of fish, which he ate in advance than returning the lure to the water. Each day, his capture dwindled till at some point, all he determined inside the lure come to be a tiny man and female. Having in no way seen this type of component, the chameleon took them to Mulungu who, after analyzing them, ordered that they be released inside the international to stroll round.

Soon sufficient, the character and lady grew in stature, and the number one detail they did modified into to strike a flint and start a fire which blazed through the woodland. Animals had been caught, killed, and cooked on the fireside. Astonished at such cruelty and barbarity, the creatures of the earth fled. The chameleon went right into a tree, followed via the spider who climbed so immoderate he reached the sky. Mulungu begged to have a look at and changed into thrown down a thread of silk upon which he climbed to enroll in the spider. Mulungu fled the earth to break out the brutality of mankind. There, he remained, such as his diploma of blame to the maligned chameleon for bringing all of this approximately.

The chameleon, as we've heard, occupies a completely unique vicinity within the mythology and superstitions of Africa, specifically a number of the Bantu. Even these days, there are few community Africans who can abide being within the proximity of a chameleon. In many instances, the notion of the chameleon's otherworldly functionality to alternate coloration and its curious mannerisms are tantamount to witchcraft, as is its characteristic due to the reality the deliverer of evil spells. It additionally brings with it the message of lack of lifestyles. A chameleon bite is reputed to have the effect of reversing suitable fortune, of turning a person right right into a woman, of causing a wound that can't heal, or of inflicting insanity. The lizard, who consists of the message of death, is likewise despised, but no longer with quite the identical irrational worry because the chameleon. The chameleon is placed inside the mythology and folklore of just about every African society. While it is nearly constantly a malevolent individual, impartial or beneficial chameleons aren't exceptional although uncommon. Chameleons can provoke infertility, insanity, and melancholy, and once they die, their bones regrow in tiny replicas of themselves.

The Swahili human beings are possibly one of the most well-known and recognizable of the African races. They are a humans of the Indian Ocean coast, stretching from the beaches of Somalia to the island of Zanzibar. Their impact on the land and people of east and major Africa has been profound, evidenced with the aid of manner of the geographic scope of the Swahili language spoken during Tanzania, Kenya, and Tanzania, and in large regions of Somalia, northern Mozambique, Rwanda, Burundi, and lots of eastern Congo. Coastal dwellers, the Swahili traditionally acted as middlemen the diverse Arab and Indian traders of the coast and the large assets of the indoors. Through lengthy exposure, the race is now predominantly Muslim, with massive interbreeding and the adoption of an Arab fashion of life, get dressed, and worship. The Swahili tale of advent is the last one in this section, and predictably, it is an African adaption of ancient Semitic beliefs influencing each the bible and the Qur'an.

At first, there has been first rate God, known as Mungu. God created a mild. At first, it was best the sunrise, but rapid enough, there came the day, with mild in all of its majestic spectrum, and He became pleased with the give up result. Then, in his omnipotence and all-information nature, he created everything that changed into, and all that would ever be. Every man or woman ever to are dwelling upon the face of the earth emerge as created at that 2d, as became each perception, movement, fortune, or misfortune until the forestall of time. First, got here the souls of the prophets, the saints, the holy men, and the religious, who would exist handiest inside the glory of Him, decreeing that their souls would live forever in slight. After this, God created the angels. Lastly, the not unusual women and men of the sector have been created. Then, got here the important factors: the Canopy, the Throne, the Pen, the Book, the Trumpet, Paradise, and Hell.

The Canopy implies the safe haven, widespread and immutable, below that is the Throne. There, God is living in glory. The Pen, which bridges the earth and sky, writes the future of mankind, and the Book is the receptacle inside which all is written. This is finished so as that each one men will recognize and recognize the law of God. The Trumpet is to announce the stop of days and the time of judgment, starting a pathway for the soul of man each to Paradise or Hellfire.

On a incredibly tons an awful lot much less orthodox plane, below the Throne of

God is a tree, referred to as the "Cedar of the End," the leaves of which may be infinite in amount, representing the lives of each character living. When a leaf falls off the tree, it's far swept up by means of manner of an angel, known as Nduli Mtwaa-roho, or the "Reaper of all Souls," and taken to its representation within the worldwide, it really is then knowledgeable that his or her time has come. The sould is then taken, supplying no respite or postpone.

Chapter 8: The Sun And The Moon

In the fundamental international of animist religion, the sun and the moon, with all of the apparent symbolism of lifestyles-giving radiance and the unchanging cycles of the seasons, are primary. Almost all traditional perception systems in Africa offer up an reason of the life of each the sun and the moon, however moreover the firmament and different imponderables of earth and sky. In times earlier than the technology of power and the enlightenment of present day era, at the identical time as the handiest mild become the sun and moon with their eternal cycle, the magical relevance of every cannot regularly be understated.

How the sun, the moon, and the stars arrived on the firmament shape a not unusual situation in the folklore of every usa of the us and people in Africa. This is truly proper in Nigeria, which grow to be and remains a favorite of anthropologists and traditional folktale lenders. This is, of path, thanks to the sheer style of Nigerian tribal manner of lifestyles, similarly to its relative accessibility in the course of the number one half of of of of the 20th century, on the identical time as there has been loads art work in accumulating the African oral way of life. Nigeria modified into part of the British Empire, and the British colonies of Africa tended to region a far greater emphasis on anthropological study than the Portuguese, French, Germans, or Belgians.

In Bantu mythology, memories of the solar and moon, in particular, usually commonly tend to run at the subject of banishment or removal thru strain. The Bushmen, or San of the Kalahari, as an example, irrespective of the truth that they are now not Bantu, supply an purpose of that the solar lived on the earth in a hut. As a outcome, his slight shone first-class within the area of its door. One day, some youngsters hurled him into the sky, and there he remained. The milky way have become shaped with the useful resource of some other mischievous infant, throwing heat ashes into the sky. In any other tale, it's far grains of shining sand. This important subject matter, that the solar changed into thrown into the sky, is echoed inside the direction of Bantu mythology, although it takes on diverse office work in unique close by corporations. The idea to that warm ashes thrown from the cooking fireside fashioned the extremely good sweep of the milky way is a few other common topic.

The Efik human beings of southeastern Nigeria offer a more tough version, taking off with the concept that Sun and Water, as separate factors, lived in a near and harmonic friendship, living at the floor of the earth. Sun often visited Water, even though the Water by no means returned the visit. When the Sun asked Water why he in no manner visited, Water replied that Sun's house become sincerely no longer massive enough to embody him. Sun scoffed at this and insisted that water come to his domestic as a vacationer. Sun, it is in all likelihood sincerely really really worth noting, modified into married to Moon, and the two lived in a huge compound. One day, as promised, Water paid a go to. With him, he added all of the sundry creatures of the sea. As Water had expected, Sun and Moon were flooded out of their domestic and crowded by means of manner of the various creatures dwelling with Water. Sun and Moon were consequently forced to interrupt out, taking secure haven inside the sky wherein they've got remained ever for the motive that.

A well-known folklore individual from West Africa, and Nigeria, specifically, is Anansi, who's normally represented as a spider. The character of Anansi end up transported during the Atlantic within the route of the generation of slavery and is, consequently, a person performing in folktales originating from the Caribbean and the Americas. One particular folktale explaining the relationship the diverse moon, stars, and solar opens with Anansi, on this event, seemingly represented in human shape, and his son, Kweku Tsin, who suffers from a excellent scarcity of food on land. Kweku Tsin leaves the home one morning, as he often does, to attempt his achievement at looking. He is successful, killing an antelope collectively with his spear. He calls his father to look. Pleased with such right fortune, Anansi instructs his son to examine over the frame of the antelope at the same time as he returns for a basket wherein to preserve the beef.

While Anansi is away, Kweku Tsin is visited through a dragon, or a monster of a few description, that breathes fireside and hungers for human flesh. Kweku Tsin flees, leaving the monster on my own with the useless antelope, in which he has no specific interest. When Anansi returns and is informed the tale with the resource of Kweku Tsin, he decides that the pair will hunt the monster. They do not should wait prolonged, because the monster smells human flesh, finds them, and consists of them away to his lair in which a exceptional many extremely good unfortunates are being held captive and looking in advance to intake.

Kweku Tsin gathers them collectively and proposes a plan of break out. The others are terrified, understanding the extremely good electricity of the monster and the loyalty of the white chicken who guards them, crowing loudly the instantaneous at which they're trying to interrupt out. Forty bags of grain are stored inside the larder, and this is scattered across the compound, for Kweku Tsin knows the bird will no longer crow if he has grain to occupy his interest. As the chicken obligingly eats, a rope is woven out of hemp, symbolizing, in all likelihood, the net of a spider. Kweku Tsin proposes hurling the give up of the rope into the sky for the gods to seize; it's miles thru this shows they'll break out.

Chapter 9: The Tale Of Aicha Kandicha

Awakening of the Shadows - The Dream of Aïcha Kandicha

The wind gently caressed the banks of the Oued Sebou, transforming the floor of the water proper right into a mirror glistening with silver reflections beneath the moonlight. In the half-mild, something became shifting, a form awakening from the depths of the water. It have end up Aïcha Kandicha, a mystical and seductive discern from Moroccan mythology, born of water, night time time and the whisper of the wind.

Aïcha Kandicha, whose call inspires a mixture of awe and understand, is a bewitchingly adorable creature. Her splendor is so impossible to withstand that she inexorably draws folks that circulate her course. Her pores and pores and pores and skin is as deep black and colorful as jet, her jet-black hair caressing her returned like a nocturnal waterfall. Her eyes are twin stars that shine with the intensity of a mirage. But at the back of this splendor lies an abyss of terror.

Its records is rooted inside the reminiscences advised inside the night, inside the douars and medinas, exceeded down from technology to technology as a warning. She is stated to appear to out of area vacationers and unwary men in desolate places, close to rivers, wells and fig timber.

The tale is going that Aïcha seduces those men with her captivating splendor and melodious voice. She attracts them into her global of illusion, wherein reality mingles with the supernatural, a international in which water and the moon's mirror are her united states. But it's far a entice. Because as soon as a person succumbs to her allure, he's doomed to a tragic stop. Aïcha Kandicha leaves him suffering from an insatiable love, an obsession that drives him to insanity and, always, dying.

Descriptions of Aisha variety from location to region, a few describing her as having goat or camel ft, others as having a fish tail or snakes for hair. These info can also moreover seem abnormal and incongruous, but they underline the duality of her man or woman: a combination of seduction and terror, attraction and repulsion.

However, it want to be said that Aïcha Kandicha's tale does no longer just serve to frighten. It additionally offers a profound mirrored photo on the relationship the diverse sexes, temptation, seduction and the outcomes of impulsive acts. Aïcha Kandicha is a powerful allegory of uncontrollable preference and the risks that expect individuals who deliver in to their passions with out questioning.

Interestingly, regardless of the fear she evokes, Aïcha Kandicha is on occasion seen as a protector of girls. In a few traditions, she is stated to punish men who abuse or cheat on their better halves. In those memories, Aïcha becomes a discern of justice, reminding guys of their responsibilities within the course of women.

This is the regular and fascinating story of Aïcha Kandicha, a creature of splendor and terror that has haunted the dreams and nightmares of the peoples of Morocco for loads of years. A tale that remains informed, a story that shimmers like a silvery reflection at the water of Oued Sebou, beneath the watchful gaze of the moon.

Deep Roots: The echo of Aïcha Kandicha

In the superb repertoire of Moroccan myths, the determine of Aïcha Kandicha occupies a place that is each bewitching and disquieting. But in which does this darkly seductive person come from? To recognize this, we want to delve into the depths of Moroccan facts, its ancient customs and wealthy cultural tapestry.

First of all, it's far honestly really well worth remembering that Morocco, like many other Maghreb nations, is a mix of different cultures and traditions. Amazighs, Arabs, Romans, Phoenicians, Andalusians - all have left their mark on Morocco's cultural landscape. These influences have woven a complex and wealthy mosaic of myths and legends, of which Aïcha Kandicha is a striking example.

The call "Aïcha Kandicha" itself is shrouded in mystery. "Aïcha" is a famous woman first call inside the Arab international, frequently related to lifestyles and vivacity. "Kandicha", but, is extra enigmatic. Some suggest that it's miles a distortion of the decision "Candace", a name given to the queens of the ancient united states of america of Kush in northeast Africa. If so, the decision need to signal a royal or divine basis for the individual.

The image of Aïcha Kandicha as a seductive temptress may be related to older archetypes of the goddess of fertility and seduction, not unusual in Mediterranean and Middle Eastern cultures. She is every so often in comparison to Lilith, a discern from Jewish mythology, called a deadly seductress.

Its association with water and desolate regions moreover shows a reference to the historic animistic beliefs of the Amazigh peoples, for whom nature spirits finished an important function. In those traditions, water is often visible as an area of transition some of the sector of the dwelling and that of the vain, an area wherein spirits can show up themselves greater without problem.

Beyond the ones feasible origins, Aïcha Kandicha is likewise thrilling for what she symbolizes. Her character serves as a metaphor for the risks of temptation and obsession, highlighting the disastrous outcomes that would give up give up end result from a loss of willpower. In a society that values moderation and energy of thoughts, Aïcha Kandicha's story is a reminder of the risks of extra and impulsivity.

At the equal time, she is likewise a image of feminine strength and independence. Her capability to seduce and dominate guys, in addition to her viable function as protector of girls, are expressions of girl authority. In a culture wherein ladies are often marginalized, Aïcha Kandicha may be seen as a undertaking to the mounted order.

Ultimately, Aïcha Kandicha is a complicated and fascinating decide, reflecting the severa layers of Moroccan lifestyle. Her tale, complete of thriller and seduction, maintains to seize humans's imaginations, and its echoes though resonate in memories informed by way of way of firelight underneath the significant starry skies of the Maghreb.

The Legend of Sidi Chamharouch

Sidi Chamharouch: Legends engraved in stone

In the coronary coronary heart of the Moroccan High Atlas, in which snow-capped peaks scratch the sky, lies an historical legend that, despite the reality that intertwined with stone and time, keeps to vibrate among individuals who tread the mountain paths. This is the tale of Sidi Chamharouch, an entity venerated through the location's population and whose cult is a complicated aggregate of Islamic traditions and ancestral Amazigh beliefs.

Sidi Chamharouch, taken into consideration the king of the djinns, is a parent of Berber mythology who enjoys superb apprehend some of the populace of the High Atlas mountains in Morocco. His legend, deeply rooted in neighborhood life-style, has been surpassed down from era to generation, inspiring an air of mystery of mystery and understand.

The tale is going that Sidi Chamharouch is a religious being dwelling within the High Atlas Mountains. He isn't always a human, however a djinn, a supernatural creature stated within the Koran. He is said to be the ruler of all djinn and to personal massive powers.

Sidi Chamharouch lives in a mountain-pinnacle cave, not an extended manner from the summit of Jbel Toubkal, the very exceptional issue in Morocco and North Africa. A massive white stone marks the entrance to his home, wherein devotees come to make offerings and ask for benefits or favors. They do not forget that Sidi Chamharouch has the electricity to answer their prayers and help them in their issues.

Legend has it that in some unspecified time in the future, a lovable more youthful girl got here to visit the shrine. She become head over heels in love with a person who did no longer note her. Desperate, she requested Sidi Chamharouch for assist. Touched with the aid of her grief, he decided to assist her. He furnished her a magical beverage that might make the person fall in love collectively together with her. The young woman followed Sidi Chamharouch's commands to the letter, and soon the man fell madly in love together along with her.

Happiness, but, was quick-lived. Another jealous man observed the reality approximately the magic beverage and determined out it to the whole village. The man who've been bewitched felt betrayed and cursed the female and Sidi Chamharouch. In reaction to this curse, Sidi Chamharouch withdrew to his cave and by no means confirmed himself to people over again. However, he continued to bestow his favors on those who honored him and sought his assist with sincerity and apprehend.

This story is one in each of many versions of the Sidi Chamharouch myth, reflecting the area's unique aggregate of Berber and Islamic traditions. The legend remains instructed and celebrated, and the shrine of Sidi Chamharouch remains a place of pilgrimage for those seeking out the blessing and assist of the king of the djinns.

Behind the Veil: The Roots and Echoes of Sidi Chamharouch

The call "Sidi Chamharouch" is itself rich in which means. "Sidi" is an Arabic honorific call meaning "my lord" or "my hold close", used to designate holy men. "Chamharouch", then again, is more enigmatic. Some translate it as "He who makes you tremble" or "He who makes you flee", a probable indication of the powers the king of the djinns is supposed to maintain.

The cult of Sidi Chamharouch is a shining instance of syncretism, in which elements from one-of-a-type traditions merge to form a unmarried exercise. On the handiest hand, we've got got got Islam, which acknowledges the life of djinns, supernatural creatures invisible to human eyes. On the alternative, we have the ancient Berber traditions that venerate the forces of nature and the spirits of the mountains.

Belief in jinn is not unusual to many Islamic cultures. Jinn are commonly appeared as impartial entities, capable of both right and evil, and are frequently invoked to provide an reason for infection or misfortune. By comparison, the veneration of a particular jinn, as in the case of Sidi Chamharouch, is rarer and shows a completely specific fusion of non secular and traditional ideals.

The Berber roots of the Sidi Chamharouch cult are more difficult to hint, however echoes of older traditions can be visible in first-rate practices. The sanctuary of Sidi Chamharouch, with its white-painted rock, conjures up the ancient Berber exercise of venerating sacred stones. Moreover, nature is an omnipresent presence within the legend of Sidi Chamharouch, recalling Amazigh ideals that venerate the earth, mountains and waters.

The legend of Sidi Chamharouch has a profound that means for those who observe it. For them, it's now not definitely an historic story, however a way of know-how the location and their area in it. The parent of Sidi Chamharouch is a photo of protection and recovery, an embodiment of ancestral expertise and divine blessing.

Chapter 10: The Myth Of Teryel

Teryel, the Shadow Ogresse

In the Maghreb's hinterland, an extended way from noisy cities and bustling souks, lurk testimonies whispered inside the darkish to people who dare to pay attention. Among those tales, that of Teryel, the ogress, aroused the greatest fear.

Teryel, a woman with shaggy hair and blood-red glowing eyes, modified into the bête noire of all Kabyle grandmothers' recollections. She haunted the forests and mountains, transferring silently via the night time time mists. Villagers attributed to it the unexplained disappearance of livestock, and once in a while even that of unwary travelers.

Teryel's recollections spread like wildfire some of the villagers, stirring worry at dusk, at the same time as shadows stretched in some unspecified time in the future of the landscape. She modified into defined as a girl of tall stature, with wild, shaggy hair that fell messily over her enormous shoulders. Her gaze modified into immoderate and hypnotic, able to paralyzing anybody who crossed it.

Teryel become stated to night meal at the flesh of animals and those she captured. She emerge as moreover feared for her sorcery skills. This is how she managed the spirits of wooded place animals, making her manner via mountains and valleys with a horde of animals at her element.

But what made the villagers shudder the most changed into Teryel's scream. A cry that sounded much like the a long way flung rumble of thunder, echoing via the mountains, reminding the villagers that the ogress modified into ever present, ever hungry.

Parents frequently used those testimonies to vicinity their disobedient youngsters, warning them of the dangers of the forest at night time time and the future they'll meet within the occasion that they came head to head with Teryel.

Despite the fear she inspired, Teryel moreover had a paranormal duration. She represented the darkish, unpredictable facet of nature, a reminder of the fragility of life and the significance of respecting the unknown forces that govern the area.

The story of Teryel, the ogress of the Maghreb, is a testomony to the ancestral fears, deep-rooted ideals and appreciate for nature that the peoples of the Maghreb have handed down from generation to era. These memories echo historic Libyan ideals, which retain to inspire recognize and worry inside the hearts of the Kabyles.

This delusion lives on these days, a specter in stories knowledgeable by way of the fireplace, an invisible however tangible presence inside the cultural panorama of the Maghreb. Teryel, the ogress, remains the embodiment of ancestral worry, a continual reminder of historical instances, engraved within the minds of these who have heard her tale.

From Tears to Cunning: Teryel's echo in Kabyle way of existence

The fantasy of Teryel, the ogress, is deeply rooted in the way of life of the Maghreb, and extra specially in the oral traditions of the Kabyle area. Although her terrifying determine symbolizes pain and worry, she also embodies foxy and astuteness, values deeply rooted in Kabyle manner of existence.

The tale of Teryel and the widow is an emblematic instance of this duality. In this story, the ogress permits a widow to weave, lifting her out of poverty. In cross returned, she asks for the widow's son. In a desperate act to store her son, the widow advises her little one to suckle the ogress' breast. The ogress, touched through the children's act, considers him her very own son and cannot convey herself to consume him.

This tale, surpassed down from generation to technology, consists of many meanings and instructions. It demonstrates the importance of cunning and intelligence in the face of chance. But it also illustrates another critical lesson of Kabyle life-style: the importance of honor and circle of relatives ties.

In this legend, Teryel is not exceptional a daunting monster, she is also a maternal figure, capable of compassion and bonding. It's this aggregate of horror and gentleness, this duality between monster and mother, that makes Teryel's character so captivating and unforgettable.

Beyond the terrifying aspect of Teryel, this story highlights the complexity of lady characters in Kabyle mythology. It underlines the energy of women, their ability to be every defensive and fearsome. The cunning of the widow and the compassion of the ogress signify girl strength and ingenuity.

Teryel's story is a testament to the richness and complexity of Kabyle way of life. It well-known the importance of recollections and myths within the transmission of values and ideals from one generation to the following. The fantasy of Teryel, the ogress, is an eloquent instance of the manner reminiscences can captivate, frighten and train, at the equal time as closing deeply rooted in the way of life and identity of a humans.

Myths of West Africa

The Legend of Shango

Shango: The Thunder of Royalty

In the bustling united states of america of the historical Yoruba, an considerable and powerful land located in what's now Nigeria, reigned a king whose reputation and legend have lived on via the centuries. His name become Shango, third Alaafin (king) of the Oyo dynasty, and his reign end up marked by using memories of electricity, hearth, thunder and a sad fall.

Shango's tale is that of a person of superb energy and ardour, a fearsome warrior king and a grasp of thunder and hearth. He end up famend for his mastery of the factors, his functionality to summon lightning and control hearth. These powers enabled him to win many battles and put in force his authority. It end up said that he must throw lightning bolts along along with his double awl, a picture of his divine strength.

But King Shango wasn't simply recounted for his strength. He modified into additionally a person of top notch appetite, well-known for his love of ladies, dance and the Bata drum. His air of thriller and infectious energy marked his reign and left an indelible mark on Yoruba way of life.

Shango's life took a tragic turn whilst his ardour and preference for energy led him to apply his mastery of the elements recklessly. In a furious rage, he unleashed a hurricane so powerful it destroyed his non-public palace and killed quite a few his topics. Overcome with regret and shame, Shango chose to keep himself, finishing his lifestyles as spectacularly as he had lived it.

But Shango's loss of lifestyles come to be not the give up of his story. After his loss of life, his people deified him and worshipped him because the god of thunder and fire. Shango's fans remember he continues to speak with the living thru lightning and thunder. He is widely known at gala's and traditional dances, wherein dancers get wearing purple and white, Shango's sacred sun shades, and dance to the frenetic beat of Bata drums.

Shango's story is a lesson in power and its limits, ambition and its downfall. It's the story of a person who reached the heights of power and success, but modified into defeated by using manner of his very very own impetuous nature. It's a tale that resonates with the human realities of weakness, guilt and regret, however furthermore offers a vision of redemption via sacrifice and divinization.

Today, loads of years after his reign, the legend of Shango continues to resonate inside the hearts and minds of his human beings. He stays a effective and respected figure, a photograph of electricity, ardour and resilience in the face of adversity. And notwithstanding the fact that his reign brought about tragedy, the flame of his spirit in spite of the truth that burns, lighting the manner for folks who are searching out to apprehend the complexity of the human condition through the pages of records.

Chapter 11: Echoes Of Sango

Legends and myths are regularly reflections of the lifestyle that spawned them, evoking the values, fears and hopes of a society. The legend of Sango, the God-King of Thunder, is deeply rooted in Yoruba manner of lifestyles, reflecting ancestral information that remains handed down from generation to technology.

Sango become the zero.33 king of Oyo, an essential metropolis-nation in ancient Yoruba. The parent of Sango is frequently related to fireplace and thunder, effective and damaging herbal forces, however moreover critical to the stableness of the arena. His affiliation with these elements displays his passionate nature, but moreover his unpredictable and sometimes detrimental person.

Sango's double awl, a photo of his divine energy, is likewise a illustration of justice and truth. Like lightning, Sango's justice is meant to strike with out caution, to punish the responsible and guard the harmless. This symbolism is applicable to Yoruba spirituality, in which Sango is invoked as a defender of the oppressed and a punisher of evil.

Dance is also an important a part of the Sango records. The God-King is frequently related to the Bata drum, a sacred musical tool utilized in non secular ceremonies. Sango dances are energetic and passionate, reflecting the critical strength and power of person of the God-King. These dances are though carried out these days at religious fairs, in which the trustworthy pay homage to Sango with the beneficial aid of dancing and gambling the Bata drum.

Sango's sacred sun shades are purple and white, symbolizing fireside and purity respectively. These colorings are regularly applied in religious rites and gala's in

Sango's honor, reminding all people of the duality of her nature and the stableness she represents.

The legend of Sango additionally tells a tale of downfall and redemption. Despite his terrific strength and recognition, Sango changed into defeated with the aid of the use of his very non-public vanity and recklessness. His tale is a reminder that power and fulfillment aren't without danger, and that even the best can fall.

Despite his tragic fate, Sango is reputable as a god and stays an critical decide in Yoruba manner of existence. His legacy is a complicated combination of power and passion, justice and vengeance, dance and music. He embodies the balance amongst energy and duty, electricity and moderation, motion and mirrored image.

Today, the legend of Sango even though resonates inside the minds of folks that inform it. It is a reminder of the energy of person, the energy of ardour, and the want for stability. But maximum of all, it is a party of the human spirit, in all its complexity, beauty and resilience.

Mami Wata, mother of the waters

The Call of the Water Mother: The Epic of Mami Wata

Once once more, we journey through the material of West African legends, guided with the useful useful resource of the echoes of recollections knowledgeable spherical the hearth. Our future, now, is the world of Mami Wata, Mother of the Waters.

It is stated that Mami Wata reigns over all our our bodies of water: from tumultuous rivers to the maximum peaceful swimming swimming swimming pools, from raging oceans to moderate rivers. Her realm is large and unfathomable, teeming with mystical creatures and hidden treasures. Her shape is as changeable because the water she governs: every so often lady, every so often serpent, on occasion each, she is usually unmatched in her splendor. Her hair is prolonged and glossy, and her eyes are as deep because the oceans.

One day, a fisherman named Tano, on the identical time as attempting to find fish to feed his village, spotted a creature within the distance. It grow to be Mami Wata, bathing in the river, her hair shining inside the twilight solar. Tano modified into so dazzled by way of her beauty that he couldn't assist looking at her. In exchange for her discretion, Mami Wata supplied him the promise of ample fishing.

Tano, amazed and worried with the aid of the usage of the use of the come across, once more to his village with nets whole of fish. His unexpected success drew the eye of his fellow fishermen, who, jealous, pressed him with questions. Tano gave in underneath strain and determined his mystery. When he lower returned to the river the following day, the waters had been calm. Mami Wata became nowhere to be visible.

The village of Tano suffered an top notch famine. The fish had disappeared from the river, and harvests had been meagre. The fisherman, feeling accountable, determined to are seeking out Mami Wata's forgiveness. He traveled for hundreds months, relentlessly searching out the Mother of Waters.

Finally, actually as he emerge as approximately to give up, Tano heard the sweet track of Mami Wata. There she became, majestic in her snake-like shape, her eyes shining like pearls inside the dark water. Tano knelt earlier than her and asked her forgiveness for revealing his mystery. Mami Wata, touched with the resource of his sincerity, conventional his repentance and promised that the river may be generous yet again.

The fisherman once more to his village with the news that Mami Wata had forgiven him. The subsequent day, the river have become teeming with fish. The village of Tano changed into saved from starvation, and the fisherman have become hailed as a hero.

Today, this legend lives on, like water that flows and now not the usage of a result in sight. It is a reminder of the respect we owe to nature, and of the outcomes of our greed. Mami Wata, the Mother of Waters, continues to observe over the waters, and those who understand them.

Reflections in Water: The Genesis of Mami Wata

The tale of Mami Wata, the Mother of Waters, is deeply rooted within the sands of time, cautiously related to African manner of existence and spirituality. The memory of her first appearance is as elusive as water slipping through the hands, however the voice of the historic storytellers is obvious and resonates in our hearts.

It is said that Mami Wata first appeared to the African people in a collective dream. It have become a time at the same time as men have been however extra youthful inside the world, the time once they started out out to recognize their region within the natural order of factors. In this dream, a snake-woman of incomparable beauty seemed on the floor of a tranquil lake, her charming gaze reflecting the information of the a long time.

When they wakened, the humans were struck via the truth of this dream. They knew it changed into no mere illusion of the napping thoughts, however a divine message. Thus, Mami Wata have come to be the father or mom of the waters, the goddess who watches over the existence that teems in lakes, rivers and oceans, and people who depend on them for survival.

Over time, respect and veneration for Mami Wata grew and spread. People came to understand that the waters are not really a useful aid to be exploited, however a important pressure to be reliable. They located out to fish without overexploiting, to navigate with out traumatic the natural balance, and to apply water without polluting it.

But Mami Wata's commands circulate past recognize for the environment. The Mother of Waters moreover teaches the value of discretion and secrecy. Like Tano, the fisherman in our tale, we have a look at that betraying a mystery have to have grave effects. And but, even in her anger, Mami Wata is a goddess of mercy, organized to forgive folks that without a doubt repent in their errors.

Today, Mami Wata stays a powerful picture in hundreds of African cultures. Her photograph may be determined in artwork, track, dance and literature, reminding us all the significance of living in harmony with nature and with our fellow people.

The myth of Mami Wata is an echo of historic instances, a vibrant tale of awareness and recognize. It invites us to look past the floor of the water, to plunge into the depths of our private humanity. For, like Mami Wata, we're formed with the aid of manner of the waters of existence, carried thru its currents and fashioned via its tides.

Yoruba Mythology: The Yoruba Pantheon

Òrúnmìlà, the God of Wisdom

The Awakening of Wisdom: The Story of Òrúnmìlà

At the start of time, the cosmos turn out to be in ordinary turmoil, with entities of divine strength growing from nothingness, each gambling a specific feature in the balance of existence. Among the ones deities stood out Òrúnmìlà, the God of Wisdom, whose story is as wealthy and complex because the threads woven into the great carpet of destiny.

Òrúnmìlà became born of Olodumare, the Supreme God in Yoruba mythology. He grow to be blessed with the prevailing of information, records and know-how. It changed into he who understood the language of birds and beasts, the secrets and techniques and techniques of vegetation and stones, and the mysterious language of future itself.

His birth grow to be a first-rate celestial event, the occasion for an unforgettable birthday party. The distinctive deities, surprised with the useful aid of the luminous radiance of his information, bowed in apprehend. Òrúnmìlà, humble in his splendid energy, promised to apply his records for the coolest of all, to guide humans along the route of future.

Throughout the some time, Òrúnmìlà proved to be a compass for the misplaced, a ray of mild in the darkness of uncertainty. He suggested kings and queens, rulers and slaves, rich and awful with same benevolence and admire. He devised the Ifa, a complex device of divination that allowed us to examine the symptoms of destiny and understand Olodumare's will.

However, the course to expertise modified into not continuously smooth. Òrúnmìlà additionally skilled challenges and trials, but he usually accompanied the route of awareness and integrity, guiding others by using way of his example. He taught the significance of truth, justice and compassion, instilling the ones values in the hearts of his lovers.

Òrúnmìlà's greatest assignment have become the high-quality drought that struck the dominion. Rivers dried up, vegetation withered and the humans suffered. Although Òrúnmìlà begged Olodumare for rain, the sky remained hopelessly blue. However, in location of giving in to despair, Òrúnmìlà used his realize-the way to discover an answer. He found a plant that might stay to inform the story without water and taught people to increase it, saving the dominion from famine.

Today, Òrúnmìlà's tale keeps to resonate via the a long term, reminding us all of the significance of attention, integrity and humility. His life is a testomony to the profound effect a single man or woman should have whilst guided by using the use of expertise and love for humanity.

From Infinite to Intimate: The Origins and Meanings of Òrúnmìlà

When plunging into the abyss of data's origins, it is not viable now not to come upon Òrúnmìlà, the Yoruba God of understanding, expertise and divination. His tale invitations us on an introspective adventure, a journey that transcends time and location, from the

Its essence is so natural, so specific, that it predates even the introduction of mankind. Òrúnmìlà is an ara orun, a primordial being who embodies the knowledge that emanates proper away from Olodumare.

Òrúnmìlà bears titles that display his deeper nature. "Igbákejì Olódùmarè", that means Olodumare's 2d-in-command, displays his immoderate rank within the pantheon of the gods. His different name, "Ẹ̀lẹ̀rìí ìpín", because of this the witness of destiny, alludes to his capability to look the thread of everyone's future.

But Òrúnmìlà's information isn't restricted to the divine sphere. He is the number one Babalawo, or "father of the call of the game", the only who is aware of the mysteries of existence and destiny. He established the priesthood of Ifá, a complicated divination exercise that uses 256 Odu, or divinatory signs and signs, each with its very own stories and prayers courting once more to the time while Òrúnmìlà walked the earth.

Òrúnmìlà is legit no longer only for his understanding, but additionally for his functionality to have an impact on people's reality extra than each different Orisha. His understanding is living now not best inside the stars and the divine geographical regions, however moreover in the coronary coronary heart and thoughts of everybody. His priesthood is open to all, women and men alike, reflecting the masculine-female stability of the universe and underlining the importance of inclusion and equality.

In ultra-contemporary global, Òrúnmìlà's have an impact on lives on. The monks and priestesses of Ifá, referred to as babalawos and iyanifas, carry on his legacy of expertise, facts and divination. Through them, Òrúnmìlà maintains to mild the course of humanity's future, guiding us all in our quest for that means and expertise.

As the story unfolds, it becomes clear that Òrúnmìlà is greater than just a mythological individual. He is the picture of humanity's eternal quest for information and records, a beacon of slight that shines in the depths of our popularity, guiding us ever onward to the truth.

Oya, Goddess of Storms

Chapter 12: The Birth Of The Storm

On the edge of the universe, wherein eternity dances with chaos, a effective entity has emerged. She emerged from the heavens, a creature as lovely as she have become indomitable. Her name grow to be Oya, the Goddess of Storms.

Oya's shipping modified into no everyday occasion. She became born from the explosive stumble upon amongst wind and fireplace, an intense fusion of ardour and power. Her first cry shook the heavens, sending waves of wind and rain across the cosmos. Even Olodumare, the precise entity, grow to be moved thru Oya's raw strength.

Oya grew up in the heavens, analyzing to understand the wind and the storm. She grow to be now not satisfactory the goddess of storms, but furthermore the father or mother of the gates a number of the global of the living and that of the useless. Her complicated, multi-faceted nature both concerned and aggravating particular deities.

Oya's story is also considered certainly certainly one of love and ardour. She became the partner of Shango, the God of Thunder and Fire. Their marriage emerge as a sight to behold, an alliance among wind and fireside, typhoon and thunder. Together, they dominated the skies, developing storms of splendid depth.

But even within the worldwide of the gods, love is not easy. Shango, attracted by way of way of the splendor of the River Goddess Oshun, ended up betraying Oya. The ache of this betrayal unleashed a hurricane of such fury in Oya that it almost destroyed the world. Shango, knowledge his mistake, returned to Oya, however she, wounded and distrustful, decided to stay impartial.

Oya is likewise appeared for her function in the adventure of souls to the afterlife. She is the father or mom of the boundary amongst life and dying, guiding the souls of the departed to their final resting location. She is often depicted with a 9-tailed fan, symbolizing her mastery over winds and storms, however additionally her electricity over the 9 degrees of the passage from existence to loss of life.

Oya's story is certainly one of energy, ardour and transformation. She is the goddess of the hurricane, but moreover the discern of the boundary among existence and death. Her tale is a lesson in pain and resilience, love and loss, and the indomitable power of nature.

Even nowadays, at the same time as a storm hits the area, the elders whisper that it's Oya dancing inside the heavens. And whilst a soul leaves this international, it's miles Oya who guides its journey to the afterlife. Her story is etched inside the heavens and the wind, an eternal reminder of nature's indomitable energy and beauty.

Wind of Change: Oya Legends and Resonances

Once upon a time, inside the coronary coronary heart of a Yoruba village, a woman named Aina changed into known for her outstanding beauty. Despite her beauty, Aina modified proper right into a proud and vain female. Conscious of her splendor, she despised the opposite women inside the village and handled them with disdain.

One day, the wind picked up, bringing with it an unknown female. It become Oya, disguised as a humble traveler. Oya requested Aina to offer her refuge for the night, however Aina laughed and refused, insulting the overseas woman for her simple look.

Angered by using manner of way of Aina's conceitedness, Oya placed out her actual form, remodeling right right into a raging hurricane. The wind blew with such force that Aina's residence become destroyed and she changed into swept away through the storm. Only after humbly requesting forgiveness modified into Aina freed from the whirlwind. This tale is a caution in opposition to delight and a reminder of the electricity of Oya, that could wreck as loads as it is able to supply existence.

Another tale tells of Oya's compassion. In a city plagued through way of using a devastating drought, human beings prayed day and night time for rain. Oya, taking note of their prayers, sent a wind that brought heavy black clouds.

Then, with a thunderous roar, she unleashed an abundance of rain, finishing the drought and bringing pleasure and treatment to the population. This story is a testament to Oya's role due to the fact the giver of existence, capable of give and take with identical depth.

The story of Oya and the two brothers is likewise famous some of the Yoruba. Two brothers, one wealthy and stingy, the opposite awful but generous, lived in the identical village. One day, an antique girl arrived in the village, asking the villagers for assist. The rich brother grew to end up her away with out a 2nd look, however the poor brother welcomed her into his home and gave her what he ought to.

The vintage woman have become out to be Oya. To thank the terrible brother, she unleashed a storm that destroyed the rich brother's issue, at the same time as the terrible brother's challenge turned into spared. Since that day, the bad brother has grow to be wealthy and rich, while the wealthy brother has determined out the hard lesson of humility and generosity. This story serves as a reminder of the importance of generosity and compassion toward others, values luxurious to Oya.

These memories, whether or not of pleasure punished, compassion rewarded, or the energy to offer lifestyles and loss of life, paint a complicated and captivating photograph of Oya. She is a pressure of nature, a raging typhoon, and a multifaceted goddess who evokes every understand and admiration. The legends of Oya are greater than only a series of myths and recollections, they may be a mirror of Yoruba way of life and a window onto an ancient information of the area.

Myths of Central Africa

The Legend of Bumba

In the Beginning : Bumba's vomit

Before lifestyles took shape, earlier than the number one slight illuminated the darkness, there was Bumba, the Supreme Being, by myself in a universe of darkness and vacancy. This is the tale of the arena's emergence from not whatever, as advised thru the Boshongo human beings of Central Africa.

In the start, Bumba changed into by myself in the darkness, a solitary presence in the limitless void. In this desolate, empty universe, Bumba felt sick, tortured through excruciating ache. It became a pain so excessive, so insufferable, that it led Bumba to do some factor surprising: he vomited.

This vomit, repugnant as it is able to appear, changed into not an act of susceptible factor or disgust, but an act of advent. For out of this vomit appeared the solar, moon and stars, illuminating the darkness for the primary time. Their slight converted the void proper right right into a spectacle of coloration and form, marking the begin of advent.

However, Bumba wasn't accomplished but. His ache hadn't subsided, and he vomited all yet again. This time, his vomit took the shape of 9 animals: the leopard, the crocodile, the turtle, the eagle, a fish, a kind of heron, a beetle, a prairie canine and in the end, a white man or woman named Loko Yima.

Every animal had a role in introduction. The leopard tore through the night with its claws, the crocodile criss-crossed the earth with its large body, the eagle soared excessive within the sky, and the fish traced rivers with its fluid movements. As for Loko Yima, he helped Bumba complete the appearance, which include records and shaping the world to make it habitable.

The turtle, but, performed a great feature. By developing a hill of sand, it delivered approximately a flood, submerging part of the earth. It changed into from this flood that the last residing beings regarded: males and females.

After that, Bumba, exhausted but glad, retired, leaving the arena he had created within the arms of his kids. He watched with love and delight as the area he had created out of his pain and pain flourished and grew, every day bringing new wonders and new memories.

So, in line with Boshongo mythology, our worldwide changed into born from an act of struggling, but moreover from an act of profound love. It's a international ordinary via pain, but additionally by using compassion and devotion, factors which can be contemplated in the lives of each creature who inhabits it.

The legend of Bumba, no matter its simplicity, is a tale of notable splendor and complexity. It reminds us that introduction is in no way an clean act, but that it is continually an act of love, sacrifice and transformation. It's a tale that, in its very essence, speaks of life itself.

Echoes and Reprints: Other Bumba Myths

The Bumba fantasy is rich and deep, and in its complexity has spawned a large number of secondary tales. These more reminiscences paint an excellent more specific picture of Boshongo mythology. They are extensions of the principle myth, losing one-of-a-kind mild at the identical scenario subjects of advent and transformation.

One of those stories tells of Mbombo, some other divine entity who appeared following Bumba's great vomit. Mbombo, in step with the story, come to be born of

Bumba's ultimate vomit, after the appearance of Loko Yima. Instead of assisting to form the arena, as Loko Yima did, Mbombo had a few different venture: she turn out to be charged with retaining the sector in stability and ensuring its harmony.

Another tale tells how Bumba, after retiring from the area, did not definitely disappear. Instead, he persisted to look at over the arena from the heavens, searching over his creations and intervening every so often even as vital. In one such intervention, he created fireplace to assist humans stay at the extended wintry climate nights. In every different, he created the wind to supply rain and make the earth fertile.

There's moreover a story about how Bumba, in a moment of outstanding sorrow, wept tears which have end up rivers and oceans. In his sadness, Bumba furthermore created track, songs and dances, that have become strategies for people to explicit their feelings and connect to him.

Another charming legend issues the animals Bumba created. According to this story, each animal acquired a selected present from Bumba. The leopard obtained power, the crocodile tenacity, the eagle eager eyesight, and the fish the ability to navigate deep water. Each of these presents had a selected motive and contributed to the order of nature.

These memories, and masses of others, boom the Bumba myth, which includes layers of complexity and intensity to the primary tale. They speak of suffering, pride, creation and destruction, stability and imbalance, and the close to relationship amongst life and loss of lifestyles.

These complementary memories to the Bumba fable remind us that each story, every myth, is a part of a larger whole. They remind us that each creature, each element of nature, has its location inside the grand scheme of lifestyles. And they remind us that, even though we're all exquisite, we are all associated with each unique and to the arena around us, in an infinite cycle of creation and transformation.

And that is in all likelihood the maximum essential message of the Bumba fable: that we are all factors of an entire, pieces of a complex and delightful puzzle. It's a message of unity and connection, a message that resonates with strength and readability via the echoes and reprises of the Bumba legend.

Chapter 13: Kongo Myths And Legends

The Song of the Nkisi: The Foundations of Myth

Deep in Central Africa, along the banks of the Congo River, lies an historical way of lifestyles, rich in myths and legends which have survived the check of time. The Kongo humans, with their centuries-vintage traditions, provide a charming account of the interplay among guy and the supernatural, wherein the visible world is but a mirrored image of the invisible international. At the coronary heart of this tradition is the concept of "Nkisi", a sacred notion that links the Kongo human beings to the past.

In Kongo cosmology, the Nkisi are spirits or invisible forces embodied in physical gadgets. These gadgets can be wooden statues, earthen pots, shells or perhaps stones. Each Nkisi possesses a totally precise power, attributed by the usage of using a specialized priest called nganga, in a complex consecration rite. Some Nkisi have the energy to heal, others to protect, and some may also even inflict curses.

Among the maximum well-known Nkisi are the so-called "Nkondi" statues. These human-sized wood statues had been respected and feared for his or her fearsome strength. The phrase "Nkondi" technique "hunter" in Kikongo, and people statues had been reputed to search out and punish people who had finished damage to the community. Nkondi have been frequently included with nails or metallic blades, every nail symbolizing a p.C. Or oath made with the statue's spirit.

A popular fable tells of a Kongo village laid low with a mysterious thief. Night after night time, food disappeared with out a trace. The community called in an nganga, who consecrated a Nkondi statue to music down the culprit. The following night time, the thief grow to be caught purple-passed thru the Nkondi spirit, who punished him for his misdeeds.

This is in which our adventure into the myths and legends of the Kongo people begins. In the subsequent sub-chapter, we're going to find out other charming memories that deliver to existence the richness and complexity of Kongo manner of life. From defensive nature spirits to cultural heroes, every tale offers a window into the deep soul of this historic lifestyle.

The Melodies of the Invisible: Supernatural Tales of the Kongo

Myths and legends are the melodies that animate cultures, portray vibrant pics of peoples and their ideals. For the Kongo human beings, those supernatural tales aren't in truth stories to bypass the time or entertain; they will be the sap that nourishes their identity and their courting with the sector. Let's dive into the maximum fascinating Kongo memories.

The fantasy of Tshibinda Ilunga is one of the most well-known epics in Kongo life-style. Tshibinda Ilunga is a legendary prince whose braveness and popularity have fashioned the identity of the Kongo human beings. According to delusion, Tshibinda, to start with from the kingdom of Luba, left his neighborhood state to marry the queen of Kongo, the stunning Lweji. Through his marriage to Lweji, Tshibinda no longer simplest united two kingdoms, however moreover delivered cultural and social improvements that converted the Kongo u . S ..

Then there may be the story of Kimpa Vita, often in assessment to Joan of Arc. Kimpa Vita end up an 18th-century prophetess who attempted to reform the Christian religion in Kongo, fusing it with conventional Kongo ideals. She claimed to be possessed through Saint Anthony of Padua and preached the want for a greater African Christian religion, less inspired by using using way of Europeans. Despite her tragic loss of life at the stake, Kimpa Vita's legacy maintains to resonate in Kongo way of lifestyles.

Finally, allow's delve into the mysterious worldwide of Kongo nature spirits. One of the most respected spirits is Nzambi a Mpungu, the ideally suited spirit who guidelines the universe. The Kongo recall that Nzambi a Mpungu created the world, but typically stay detached from human affairs. However, in the direction of herbal disasters or number one crises, the Kongo humans invoke Nzambi a Mpungu for assist and safety.

Each myth, each legend, is a word in the symphony of African cultures, a melody that resonates via the some time, maintaining the awareness of our ancestors and illuminating our route to the future. As we near this financial ruin, we take with us the reminiscences of the Kongo people, echoes of the beyond that shape the identification of Africa nowadays.

Myths of East Africa

The Legend of Nandi Bear

The Myth of the Nandi Bear

Deep inside the forests of Kenya, in which the sounds of civilization appear a much off whisper, a creature haunts the spirits of the indigenous peoples. His name is Chemosit, however he is likewise called Nandi Bear, a specter that hovers over the Rift Mountains.

According to close by using folklore, the Nandi Bear is a frightening creature, an animal the size of a bear however with the appearance of a hyena, sharp claws and eyes that glow inside the darkness of the African night time. It has the popularity of being an insatiable predator, feeding especially on the brains of its patients.

The brilliant-known tale of the Nandi Bear is that of the historical warrior Akai. At the time, Nandi Bear assaults had turn out to be so common that villagers lived in consistent fear. Brave and decided, Akai decided to put an surrender to this terror. Armed with a spear and his braveness, he spark off in the route of the Nandi Bear's lair.

The battle that found have become fierce. Akai fought the creature with bravery and talent. Every time the Nandi Bear tried to assault him, Akai controlled to live away from and counter-assault. Finally, after a fierce struggle, Akai managed to pierce the beast's coronary coronary heart with his spear, putting an stop to the Nandi Bear's reign of terror.

But the legend of the Nandi Bear would possibly not give up with the creature's loss of existence. On the alternative, it keeps to dangle-out the creativeness of the peoples of East Africa. Stories of encounters with the Nandi Bear abound, reinforcing the belief that the creature, or likely its descendants, maintains to hang-out the Rift Mountains.

In the darkness of the bush, even as the wind howls and the leaves rustle, the Nandi Bear stays a tangible presence, a caution toward the dangers that lurk inside the darkness. For the people of this place, the Nandi Bear is an inseparable a part of their way of lifestyles and folklore, a shadow that reminds us that the boundary among guy and barren place is frequently extra tenuous than it seems.

Despite its horrifying nature, the legend of the Nandi Bear is also a reminder of the significance of courage inside the face of adversity. The Akai myth is a tale of formidable and backbone, characteristics which is probably as crucial nowadays as they had been inside the days of the historical warriors. And on the identical time as most folks will never move paths with a Nandi Bear, all people face our very very own "beasts", challenges that name for our courage and treatment.

The legend of Nandi Bear is a first rate deal more than a easy horror tale. It's a lesson in courage and perseverance, a metaphor for the challenges everybody face in life. It's a fable that, via the centuries, maintains to resonate within the hearts and minds of the people of East Africa.

In the Shadow's Footsteps: More memories from Nandi Bear

Beyond Akai's well-known warfare with the Nandi Bear, the creature has left its mark on many different East African testimonies. These recollections are handed down from generation to era, feeding the legend and developing a wealthy tapestry of folklore across the creature.

One such story tells of a greater youthful hunter named Jengo's encounter with the Nandi Bear. While chasing an antelope via the bush, Jengo noticed a tall figure moving through the timber. Curious, he followed the discern to a clearing wherein he located the Nandi Bear. Instead of fleeing, Jengo defended his territory, brandishing his bow and arrow with unshakeable self-discipline. Impressed by way of his braveness, the beast left him on my own and disappeared into the woodland. Jengo another time to his village, his bravery having earned the honor of all.

Another tale tells of a female named Nyala, whose village have turn out to be terrorized with the resource of using the Nandi Bear. The villagers lived in normal worry, going out only ultimately of the day and barricading their houses at night time. However, Nyala, a decided mom, decided to guard her own family and her village. One night, she set a trap for the Nandi Bear, placing a clay pot whole of honey in a leaf-covered pit. The scent of honey attracted the Nandi Bear, who fell into the entice. In the early hours of the morning, Nyala and the opportunity villagers located the imprisoned beast and managed to chase it faraway from their village. Nyala's bravery has end up a image of braveness for her humans.

These stories, and plenty of others, testify to the deep bond between the humans of East Africa and the character that surrounds them. The Nandi Bear is not only a frightening creature, it's also a picture of nature's wild strength and human bravery in the face of adversity.

Despite its frightening look and terrifying popularity, the Nandi Bear has emerge as a applicable individual in East African folklore, a meditated picture of the intimate connection amongst man and nature. The memories that surround it are a combination of worry, recognize and fascination, a example of the complexity of our dating with the natural worldwide.

The legend of the Nandi Bear lives on in the hearts and minds of the people of East Africa. Through those tales, the creature interferes in dreams and nightmares, a continual presence that recollects the mysteries of nature and the power of human courage. The Nandi Bear is a shadow within the bush, a spectre in the night time time time, but additionally a image of the indomitable power of nature and the human spirit.

The Nyaminyami Story

The Awakening of the River Snake

East Africa's rugged landscape is domestic to a rich sort of myths and legends, every with its very personal glint of strangeness and splendor. Among them is the gripping story of Nyaminyami, the God of the Zambezi River. A serpent-like deity whose story transports us into the depths of intrigue, vengeance and eternal love.

In the start, the Zambezi River changed right into a peaceful region, a shimmering ribbon of blue running thru the earth. It modified into the domain of Nyaminyami and his loved, divine snake-like creatures whose our our bodies coiled and coiled across the river. They were the guardians of the river and its populace, shielding the fish, the crocodiles and the individuals who lived on its banks.

However, the couple's quiet happiness end up shattered at the same time as the men built the Kariba dam. The dam separated Nyaminyami from his associate, leaving her on the thing of Lake Kariba, while Nyaminyami himself become stranded downstream. Furious and distraught, Nyaminyami provoked terrible floods and storms in a decided attempt to break the dam and reunite alongside together with his partner.

Every one year, for the duration of the wet season, Nyaminyami unleashes his wrath at the dam, causing floods and storms in an try to interrupt it. Each time, however, the dam resists, and Nyaminyami is compelled to retreat, leaving chaos and destruction in his wake.

The Tonga people, who stay along the Zambezi River, tell the story of Nyaminyami with a combination of awe and respect. They recognize that Nyaminyami is a powerful god, capable of inflicting notable floods and destroying whole villages. However, additionally they recognize that Nyaminyami is a god of affection, who fights to discover his preferred. For the Tonga, Nyaminyami is the embodiment of the river's wild, untamed nature, in addition to the destructive electricity of affection.

The legend of Nyaminyami is greater than only a tale of divine wrath and out of vicinity love. It's a tale approximately the bond amongst guy and nature, and the way that bond can be broken with the aid of way of human intervention. It's a reminder of the energy of nature and the need to live in concord with it.

In the legend of Nyaminyami, we see the tragedy of out of place love, the awful power of anger and the not possible to resist strain of nature. It's a story that resonates with the echoes of ardour, disappointment and resolution, a story that is engraved within the heart and soul of anybody who lives along the Zambezi River.

Beyond the Flood: Echoes of Nyaminyami

The legend of Nyaminyami, the serpent-like deity of the Zambezi River, is rich and complicated. It is going an prolonged manner beyond the preliminary tale of Nyaminyami's tragic separation from his loved by means of the Kariba Dam. The legend grows and spreads, encompassing unique local testimonies and traditions, permeating the cultural panorama of East Africa with deep and transferring resonances.

One of these testimonies recounts the shipping of the number one Tonga peoples. It says that when Nyaminyami added approximately the number one fantastic flood in retaliation for the development of the Kariba dam, couples were separated and swept away by way of the raging waters. When the waters subsided, those people determined themselves scattered along the river. They formed the number one Tonga villages, establishing a society that lives in near concord with nature and respects the electricity of Nyaminyami.

Another story describes how Nyaminyami used her electricity to help humans. In a year of devastating drought, the Tonga human beings located themselves with out food and without desire. In their desperation, they have grow to be to Nyaminyami. Recognizing their respect and devotion, Nyaminyami brought on a flood which, on the identical time as destroying their homes, furthermore added fish and distinctive food in abundance. So, even in his anger, Nyaminyami also can convey lifestyles.

The Legend of Nyaminyami is also a tale of justice and revenge. One story tells of a cruel and grasping man who exploited others to complement himself. He had built a huge residence thru the river, dismissing warnings that he have become on Nyaminyami land. One night time time, a outstanding flood came, washing away the residence and the grasping guy. It is stated that this modified into Nyaminyami, dishing out justice for those who could not defend themselves.

www.ingramcontent.com/pod-product-compliance
Lightning Source LLC
Chambersburg PA
CBHW071331120626
46546CB00002D/523